Plotting the Character-Driven Novel

Plotting the Character-Driven Novel

Linda Rodriguez

Scapegoat Press
Kansas City, Missouri

Scapegoat Press
P.O. Box 410962
Kansas City, Missouri 64141
www.scapegoatpress.com

ISBN 978-0979129155

"The question is, What's in you that you can free up? How to say everything you know?"

— Jonathan Lethem

Acknowledgments

As always when I finish a book, I am faced with how much I owe to so many people who have helped and encouraged me through the years. With this book about the writing process, I am more aware of this than usual.

First of all, to those teachers through the years who have helped me to become the writer and teacher that I am—Mildred Sykes, James McKinley, Janet Burroway, Robert Stewart, and most of all, Sandra Cisneros, who has taught me through her example, her mentoring, and her friendship, as well as in the Macondo Workshop.

I must also thank many of my writer friends who have engaged with me in long and short discussions of the craft that have set off chains of ideas and insights in my head—Marjorie Agosín, Ruth Behar, Sally Berneathy, Mitch Bryan, Lucha Corpi, Deborah Crombie, Diane Glancy, Debra Goldstein, Frank Higgins, Lorraine Lopez, Deborah Miranda, Jacquelyn Mitchard, Nancy Pickard, Trish Reeves, Hank Phillippi Ryan, Julia Spencer-Fleming, Sergio Troncoso, and Luis Alberto Urrea. Also, thanks go to members of my long-time novel writing group—Deborah Shouse, Jacqueline Guidry, Judith Fertig, and Robin Silverman.

I am extremely grateful to ArtsKC Regional Arts Council, which has supported my work throughout the years with grants and other recognition.

I am always grateful for my husband, and true partner in life Ben Furnish, and to all my family, but especially with this book, I must give a special thank-you to my oldest son, Christopher Niles Rodriguez, who has been of particular assistance in bringing this course to book form.

Contents

How to Use This Book

Writing a novel requires several things—time, motivation, the willingness to keep learning the craft of fiction, and an ability or process to access your creative thoughts. We'll deal with the first two in this chapter briefly since they're mostly beyond the purview of this book, and the rest of the book will concern itself with elements of the craft of fiction and a process for accessing your own inner knowledge of your novel by freewriting, brainstorming by yourself, and thinking on paper. I will be including samples of actual work documents I have used with this process to create published novels in order to give you examples of how these techniques and tools work—and also to show that behind those perfect books you pick up at the bookstore lies a great deal of hard work, messy process, and flailing around. This book is designed to help you keep the flailing around to the minimum.

The craft of fiction involves a number of separate elements, such as characterization, scene structure, pacing, dialogue, conflict, transitions, handling needed exposition, narrative structure, emotional tension, setting or background, suspense, style, and many more. It has been my experience as a working writer that most of these elements connect and overlap to the point that dealing with them separately is not necessarily useful. In this book, we will learn how to make them work together to create an integrated whole.

I will share with you a system for plotting a good character-driven novel that I have developed over the years through a lot of trial and error. My hope is that I can help you to avoid a lot of those errors I had to make along the way and make your path to a well-written novel smoother. However, this book will not show you how to get an agent or a publisher. This book is purely about writing the best novel you can write—and if you do that, your chances of achieving representation or publication are much higher. So for the duration, set aside all those desires for publication and mega-sales and fame and fortune. Let's concentrate on writing a novel where the characters are fully realized and the narrative and action all derive from the motivations of those characters.

Writing Is Thinking on Paper

In this book, we will use the technique of freewriting in many ways—as freewriting itself, as a kind of brainstorming by yourself on paper, as a rapid listing tool, and as what I call *thinking on paper*, a free-form exercise in analysis, questioning, and creating possible alternative solutions. Freewriting is the technique that I've found most helpful for the kind of deep character work that is the basis of this method. You may be familiar with it from one of the many writing teachers who teach it now, each calling it something different such as morning pages or timed writing. Or you may less commonly know it from the woman who first started it in the 1930s, Dorothea Brande, or the great writing teacher and novelist, John Gardner, who brought her work back to the attention of writers in the second half of the 20th century (including all those who now teach it as their own).

For freewriting, you will set a timer for ten or more minutes and write about anything or, in our case, on a set topic without stopping until the timer goes off. This allows your brain to get out all the conscious thoughts on that topic and then to dig into the riches your unconscious has learned or created on the same subject. I suggest ten minutes for your first session as you learn to use the technique, but you will want to increase that time of each session as rapidly as you can. The longer you work in one session of freewriting (up to the point of fatigue), the more successful that session will probably be. The conscious mind becomes bored with trying to control and obstruct the freewriting over time and loosens its vise grip on your mind, allowing you to access what you already know or have created within your unconscious mind.

I have stressed so heavily that you do this in writing because it is too easy to believe we are thinking our way through something, only to find, when we have to write that scene or book, that we were really only daydreaming fitfully about it. Writing is thinking on paper. The very act of writing out our questions and thoughts leads us to answers and new possibilities. Successful speculative fiction writer, Scott Westerfeld, has explained it the best I've seen yet—"You see, paper is magic: Making marks on it changes your brain. So, don't sit around trying to think your way out of problems, write your way out of them. The best place to find answers is on a piece of paper or a glowing phosphorus screen."

When freewriting, you can write by hand in a notebook or type it into your word-processing program. Choose whichever method works best for you. You might try each method and compare the results you get with both of them before settling on one method. Although I do most of my work, including freewriting, on the compute, I have noticed that, when I'm particularly stuck and words refuse to flow, I get better results with an old-fashioned pen and notebook or blank paper.

To Find Time to Write Your Novel, You Must Make Time to Write

How do you find time to write the novels which are your vocation in the midst of job and career demands, family and housework demands, community and societal demands? When everyone else expects so much from you that there's nothing left for your own dreams, what can you do about it?

First, we have to change our terminology from "finding time to write" to "making time to write." The sad truth is that no one finds time to write. There aren't big pockets of time just lying around waiting to be picked up and used in most of our lives. For most of us, we'll have to give up some comfort or pleasure to make real time to write—in some cases, to make any bits of time to write at all.

The first step is to make the decision to own your own life. Time is not a commodity—the time we're talking about is the substance of your life. When it's gone, so are you. If you want to write anything, you have to claim your own life and find out what you want.

How do you find those pieces of time and the regular schedule for writing that leads to a body of work? The trick is to create order and make a tourniquet for a time hemorrhage, but first you must destroy all of those 'shoulds' and 'what will people thinks' that are standing in your way. Make it easy on yourself by asking for help and accepting help when it's offered to you. Take the time to de-stress. When you're not frazzled by stress, you'll find it easier to set limits and boundaries and hold to them.

Whenever you find your desk or day becoming chaotic, take time to reorganize. It will repay in more time that you can steal for your illicit love affair with the novel. To make sure you stay on track with those things that absolutely must be done, make a brief list of the way your time was spent at the end of each day and week. Check it for places where you abandoned time reserved for writing or other truly necessary tasks to engage with lower priority urgencies or comfort activities. After a disastrous day, sit down with a notebook and figure out how to handle things differently if you face the same situations again. Review the situation and just what happened step by step, pinpointing the spot(s) at which you could and should have made a different decision or taken a stand against someone else's urgency with your time. Figure out a strategy for dealing with this situation when it next arises, and write it down. Then forget the day and relax.

Worrying about the myriad things, some great but most small to tiny, that we must take care of wears us down. When you find yourself doing this rather than being able to write or revise the passage you want to work on, keep an ongoing master list and write down each task or obligation the moment you think about it. Get it out of your head and onto paper to free your mind and stop the energy drain. Then, later, you can decide which tasks can be delegated to someone else and arrange the remaining tasks in the order that will allow them to be done quickest and most easily.

We can also free up energy by developing habits and systems to take care of the mindless stuff. We already do this every day, brushing teeth, driving to work, without having to make decisions for each tiny action that comprises these tasks. Develop a system for handling things that recur, and stick with it for twenty-one days. Then it will be a habit, and you can forget it and set your mind free to be more creative.

Much time use is sheer habit. Work smarter. Find the ways in which you want and need to spend time. Steal those minutes and hours from low-priority tasks. Break down everything on your to-do list into small tasks and estimate the minimum time to accomplish them. (Double all time estimates!) Schedule into your calendar. If they won't all fit in the time allotted, then something must go. Nothing is fixed in stone--renegotiate and eliminate whatever you can. Of the rest, what can you successfully delegate? It pays to invest time (and money, if possible) in training someone to do it.

Become assertive. Don't be afraid to approach someone with a request, and don't take it personally if they refuse you. Learn to say 'no' kindly and firmly and to receive a 'no' without letting it affect your self-esteem or your relationship. Be secure.

Author of many published novels and teacher of writing, Holly Lisle, says it the best way I've ever seen it. "Realize that real writers who write multiple books and who make a living at it have systems they use. A process for brainstorming, a consistent way of outlining a story, a certain number of words or pages a day, a way of plotting, a way of revising, a way of finishing. Writing is work. It doesn't fall out of your head by magic. It doesn't just happen because you want it to."

Motivating Yourself to Write in the Time You've Created

The next trick is to motivate yourself to actually write in that time slot you've created. Most of us find it easier to disappoint ourselves than to disappoint other people, so if you can find a buddy or partner to help keep you accountable, that's a great way to overcome that difficulty. Perhaps you two can call, text, or email each other every writing day with goals before your writing time and what you accomplished after that time is over. Or a group of writer friends on Facebook can do this for each other. I know a number of writers who post their day's time spent writing or page totals on Facebook, and get lots of positive feedback from their writer friends for it—or consolation if they've missed their goal.

It's also important to set regular rewards for yourself for completing planned segments of writing tasks. Putting your feet up with a cup of tea and a special treat. Spending time reading a book you've wanted to read. Buying yourself a book you want. Buying nice pens or blank notebooks or whatever desk/office gizmo you've been wanting or needing. Buying materials you've wanted for a craft project and--as a later reward--giving yourself time to work on that project. Lunch with one or more friends. Make a list of small, medium, and large rewards for fulfilling various writing commitments.

Also, schedule some creative refill time into each week and month. Take a walking or library or bookstore or art gallery or museum break every week, even if it's only for thirty minutes. Take a nice blank book (one of your rewards) and a nice pen (another reward) and visit a lake, park, nature preserve, or riverside, just walking and sitting and writing with no stated purpose. Describe in writing what you see, what you feel, what you're thinking, what you want to write someday or otherwise do someday.

If you're serious about writing, reclaim your power. Would you treat your car the way you treat yourself? No, you would make sure it had as much quality fuel as it needed. You would buy new tires for it when they were needed. You would check its oil and get it regular tune-ups and other routine maintenance. You would do all of this because you know these things are important to keep it functioning at its peak. Show yourself as much consideration as you do your car. No car will run on empty, and neither do writers.

Make time to remember how to dream, and make time to bring those dreams into reality. Visualize your successful life as a writer, and then plan that change. Exercise your change muscles first by making small, unimportant, non-threatening changes in private areas. Learn to make a habit of changing things you are unhappy with—in your job, your home, your relationships, yourself. Envision the life you want to lead. Write it down. Check in with it often. Analyze problems. Get back on the horse when you fall off, and fix the problems that led you to fumble your plans or work routine. It's always an ongoing process. No one's perfect, but the only way you can truly fail is if you stop for good.

Learning to Read as a Writer

A serious writer should be reading all the time. Buy books, so you can reread and mark them up, figuring out how their writers do the incredible things they do and how they made the mistakes they made that you want to avoid. Read the first time the way any reader does—for enjoyment and delight, to find out what happens next. Then, read over and over—very slowly. Read and ponder. Read like a writer reads—for technique. These writers are your teachers—for the cheap cost of a book, $30 at the max for a hardback, a lot less for a paperback. If you're strapped for cash, pick up copies at the used bookstore.

Learn everything you can from them. Learn from the best. Then go practice some of those good techniques in your own work. You can do this quietly in bits and pieces of time without having to go away anywhere. You're a writer. Think on paper.

There are lots of areas in our life where we need to step out of our comfort zones in order to grow and achieve our goals. It can be difficult to do this because it feels so weird outside of the spaces where we're accustomed to spending time, and that leads to discomfort. Most of us, however, have learned that we have to stretch ourselves at times. But we seldom do this in our reading. Teachers may have made us read things we didn't care for, but on our own—if we read at all!—we read only what we're comfortable with.

Writers must read. We must read for enjoyment and delight and relaxation. We must read to stay up with what's going on in our field. Above all, we must read to learn—and that involves sometimes leaving the warm cocoon of blankets and stepping out onto the cold floor of books and authors we might never choose for enjoyment.

We tend to read people who write like we do, who believe what we believe, who have the same style. It's natural and normal—like looking in the mirror. I write accessible poetry with a narrative behind it. When I turn to poetry, won't I read the same thing? I did. I still do. Reading Linda Hogan or Mary Oliver is like looking in the mirror at myself—years younger, many pounds thinner, and much more beautiful, it's true—but an idealized self. My favorite kind of crime novels tends to be novels that focus on character, complex plots, and fine writing. I could recognize the artistry of good comic, pulp hardboiled, and puzzle crime novels, but I tended not to read those, except when I had to, because they weren't "my" crime novels. But there were things for me to learn from these writers who didn't write "my" books—exactly because they wrote a different style of book that required different skills. I could learn things from them that I couldn't learn from someone just like me.

This is not just applicable to novels, either. You may only want to write fiction or narrative nonfiction, so why would you read poetry? As a matter of fact, many acclaimed writers of fiction, including some bestselling authors of commercial fiction like Deborah Crombie and Julia Spencer-Fleming, start or end many of their days reading poetry because they want to learn the skills of precise word choice, compression, verbal musicality, and many others they can learn from poets who've worked for years to be masters of those skills. The prose writers believe they can use those skills profitably in their own novels, stories, and narrative nonfiction.

Will all writers offer examples of all of these skills? Of course not. You must search out the best in each style or school. You always want to learn from the best. Where else can you as a writer turn to learn from your reading? Well, what do you want to learn?

Is narrative structure and plot your weakness? Do you never have any conflict in your stories or books? Look to the best of mystery fiction. These are the masters of narrative structure and plot. A good mystery has to have the plot of what really happened and then the plot of the unraveling and discovery of what really happened. Good mysteries have to have dramatic structures that are tied into strong characterization, motivation, lots of conflict, and suspense. Good examples can be found in authors like Nancy Pickard, Paul Doiron, Julia Spencer-Fleming, Michael Connolly, Margaret Maron, and Louise Penny.

Are you unable to build a believable, engrossing background for your characters? Do your characters wander in a void? The best writers in science fiction and fantasy excel in world-building—making a fictional world so believable in its details that it will draw the reader in as if it were a real place. They must make worlds that never existed outside their heads into places that readers can see and believe in. *Game of Thrones*, anyone? Good places to start here are C.J. Cherryh, Ursula K. LeGuin, Kate Elliott, Octavia Butler, and N.K. Jemison.

Reading as a writer can help you with any writing problem you have (except the constants of procrastination and lack of confidence). If your current problem is transitions, find writers who write fabulous transitions, even if you don't like the rest of their work. They may be literary writers or writers in some commercial genre, but they write transitions that really work. Learn from them. Take apart the way they write transitions. Identify their techniques. Then practice them. This kind of reading to identify and break down skill and technique is a valuable tool for any writer. Good writers have books that are underlined, highlighted, and have notes scribbled in them.

A second kind of reading as a writer is reading to learn other ways of thinking and seeing the world. If we keep to our circumscribed lives, how can we realistically create characters who are different from ourselves? I am a screening judge for several national literary contests and see way too many book manuscripts where everyone in the whole book is the same—a twenty-to-thirty-something graduate student (even if they're not in school). A Native American grandmother is written from the perspective of a twenty-to-thirty-something graduate student and lies dead on the page.

Does this mean a twenty-to-thirty-something graduate student can't/shouldn't try to write a Native American grandmother? No, but she or he might try reading things written by Native Americans and grandmothers from the perspective of real Native Americans and real grandmothers first. Otherwise, this character will be built from his/her preconceived notions—stereotypes and prejudices—of what a Native American grandmother is and will never rise up alive on the page.

How can we learn if we only read people who think and write the same way we do? As writers, we need to use our reading to add breadth to our experiences. To do that, we must read people who are different from us—people who write differently and think differently, people who have had different experiences in life from ours. There is a whole world of books out there by people whose whole experience of life has been different from yours. At one time, the only books to be found were written by wealthy educated European white men. Now, we can read and learn from the experiences of working-class Irish plumbers, overachieving Chinese law professor mothers, Filipino cab drivers, and African

American choreographers. Biographies, autobiographies, and memoirs are a wonderful resource for this broadening of experience, as are poetry and fiction by these diverse authors. Your characters will thank you, as will your readers.

But what if you don't know where to look to find the books that will help you learn new techniques and new worlds? Ask your librarian. Most of them have their jobs because they love books. All of them are knowledgeable about books.

Don't always read only the people who look like you, sound like you, and write like you, whose skills, backgrounds and experiences are just like your own. You won't find anything to stretch your understanding or increase your skills there. Do everything you can to widen your perspective on the world. It will all make you a better writer. You'll know you're a real writer when all your mirrors turn into windows.

It All Starts With Character

I have often told students that, if they want to learn to plot, they should read well-written mystery novels. Mysteries are famous for their robust narrative structures and intricate plotting. Their authors learn to use suspense and pacing to keep readers turning the page, and they are experts at handling character secrets and revelations. Depending on the type of crime novel it is, a mystery writer will become adept at handling the parceling out of information in small amounts just as it is needed and the placing of clues and red herrings.

Consequently, aspiring mystery writers worry more than anything about how they can learn to plot their novels. But all great plot in any genre, including literary novels, springs from character and the motivations each character has for taking or not taking any particular action. In this book, you will learn how to use character as the springboard to a strong plot that draws its complexity from the motivations of its characters in whatever genre you desire to write.

What are the hidden fears and desires of each major character? Does your character desperately want the top executive position within a major corporation or a major political office? Instead does your character long for romantic love and lifelong commitment, or is she driven by sexual desire for as many attractive people as she can seduce? Is he afraid of snakes like Indiana Jones, whose author used that fear to push him to the limit in *The Raiders of the Lost Ark*? Is she afraid of enclosed spaces like Anna Pigeon, whose author made her descend into a narrow, deep cave to save the life of a dear friend in *Blind Descent*? Does your character fear losing his father's respect? Is she most afraid of something terrible happening to her adored child?

What happens with your character and plot when these desires are frustrated or these fears are triggered? If someone hinders his chances for the corporate CEO position, what will he do? If she faces a well-funded political opponent who is loved by the media and the party, how will she respond? If the woman he loves is swept off her feet by another man, will he try to win her back or will he try to sabotage her new relationship? If someone tries to pressure her into a monogamous relationship, will she be unfaithful or run away? If he's forced to confront a pit of snakes or give up his greatest ambition, what will he do? If she's forced to wriggle through a long, tight tunnel to get out of a cave and save her and her friend's life, will she make herself do it or simply give up? If his father learns something about him that causes him to hold his son in contempt, how will that son react? If her child is kidnapped or held hostage, will the normally timid, inexperienced mother try her own rescue when no one else will help?

How do these different desires and fears intersect and conflict with one another within the same character and among different characters?

Another way to motivate a character's actions and, thus, your plot is to use secrets. Everyone, even the most pure and innocent among us, has secrets, perhaps even from that person's own conscious awareness. What are the secrets this character is hiding from others or even from himself or herself?

Related to secrets are the things a character is ashamed of. Often, these are guilty secrets—things he has done or she has experienced—but all too frequently, people are also ashamed of aspects of their appearance, family history, culture, heritage, or personality that they have little or no control or responsibility for.

How do you learn these things about your characters? The truth of that is that, deep inside yourself, you already know all of this about your created people, so you simply ask your characters to tell you all their secrets, fears, and desires. This character will tell you everything you want to know about herself or himself if given the chance.

Through asking these kinds of questions of your characters on paper and allowing them to answer on paper, you will learn to create an exciting and complex plot, building from the integrity of the characters you create.

You can sit down and create an artificial narrative structure by listing one exciting plot event after another. First, a man with a gun shows up and threatens the protagonist. Next, the protagonist chases the man with the gun on foot, and just as he almost catches him, someone unseen knocks him out. The protagonist comes to and heads back to his car to drive back to his office, only to find on the freeway that his brake lines have been cut. Cue daredevil driving in and out of traffic trying to avoid being killed since he can't slow his car down. He takes an exit that leads into the suburbs where he drives the car into a park pond so he can survive the crash.

You can continue in this line with thrilling scenes one after another through the book and end with a giant pyrotechnic climax where the protagonist saves the entire world from destruction. If you sit down to write the book from this outline, however, you will find it dead on the page. It doesn't matter how many high-action scenes you plan or write. If no one knows or cares about your people, they will all fall flat. If you don't show the reader why this goal matters to your protagonist or why your antagonist needs to make sure your protagonist fails and preferably dies, nothing that happens on the page will be believable.

Developing and Exploring Your Protagonist through Freewriting

I believe, with F. Scott Fitzgerald, that character is plot and plot is character. So we begin our work with character and by exploring and developing that character in writing. The first character of your novel to develop is your protagonist. This is the character your reader will identify with and root for as she faces and struggles to overcome obstacles in the path toward her desperately desired goal. If this character is not deeply developed and realized on the page, your novel will not succeed, no matter how many action scenes you pile on top each other, no matter how dazzling and pyrotechnic the climax. Readers don't necessarily have to like your protagonist, but they have to be truly interested in him and invested in seeing him succeed.

How do you create such a protagonist? You already are creating this character within your unconscious mind as you mull over your book. The trick is to bring that information you already have and are currently creating about your protagonist up to the surface and make it accessible to your conscious mind. The freewriting technique I explained in the first chapter, **How to Use This Book**, will help you to gain that access to the creative riches of your unconscious mind.

This exercise will give you a chance to work with this technique if you never have before and to set some basics of that character in place before we start looking at setting and story concept.

Exercise 1: Set a timer and ask yourself on paper the

following questions. Give yourself at least 10 minutes for each question. Remember, you must keep that pen or cursor moving until the timer goes off.

A.   Before your book opens, what makes your protagonist different from other people? What sets her/him apart and possibly isolates her/him?

B.   What is your protagonist's primary strength or asset? Does the world around your protagonist recognize and value this quality, or is it unappreciated?

C.   How does this advantage or strength cause problems for your protagonist? Does s/he tend to rely on it too much? Does it lead her/him into risky situations or lead to her/him being taken advantage of by others?

Coming Up With a Killer Concept

Which comes first? Location, situation, or character? The truth is that your initial seed for your novel can come from any one of these, but you will soon enough have to bring in the other two before you can have a truly exciting concept for the book. We're going to talk about character-driven plotting in this course, but your character has to be rooted in a place (or be challenged by a new or hostile place), and a situation has to be set up that provides a major challenge to your character. A character floating in empty white space or mythical TV-nowhere land is not going to interest a reader. Neither is a character whose situation offers no problems, challenges, threats, or conflict. Whether you begin with a fascinating character, an interesting location, or a dramatic situation, one piece simply won't be enough all by itself.

You must have the location and background, the initial situation, and the protagonist solidly in mind before you can really start developing your story. Once you have at least the beginnings of all three of those aspects, then you can use character subjected to the stresses and limitations of the situation and place to plot your novel.

Where do we come up with ideas for any or all of these three aspects of story? The first step is to be open to the ideas all around us. My husband has been going to enough mystery writers conferences and reading so many books that my friends have published that he's almost as good as I am now about spotting a great location to find a body or have a showdown or set a mystery. (Yes, our conversations don't bear overhearing—"It's a perfect spot for an ambush," "If you dumped a body back in there, it wouldn't be found until some of those kids over there came nosing around.") We will witness an awkward conversation or argument between people at a coffee shop or restaurant—be unwilling eavesdroppers to a loud cell phone argument—and speculate about how that state of affairs could provide motive for murder and a volatile situation ready for a precipitating incident.

Pay attention to the people around you, their conversations and their actions. Ask, "What if?" Those two little words are the most valuable tools of the novelist at the beginning of the book. What if a Puritan woman whose husband was gone had an illicit love affair and got pregnant? What if a crazed whaling captain decided to go after the monster whale that took off his leg? What if a poor and plain but intelligent and strong-willed girl in Victorian England refused to be a victim and eventually wound up the governess at a scary mansion for a harsh employer with whom she fell in love? What if scientists could recreate living dinosaurs from the DNA in prehistoric dinosaur bones? What if a giant white shark began to terrorize a beach resort town? All those novels and movies arose from writers asking themselves, "What if?"

You never know when you will encounter that grain of sand around which you can build the pearl of character and/ or situation. Henry James once famously said, "Try to be one of the people on whom nothing is lost." And remember what F. Scott Fitzgerald said, "Character is plot, plot is character."

Keep notebooks always with you to capture ideas and bits of description of places, characters, or situations you see or overhear. Keep these large and small notebooks by your bed, in your purse or pocket, inside your cell phone or tablet, in your briefcase/bookbag, on your laptop or desktop computer, beside all the chairs in which you regularly sit. Use them also to note down interesting ideas and bits from books that you read.

Create an idea file with newspaper articles, internet items, and stories you hear from others. Some of my friends and family send me interesting items of news or research they come across. Even if it's not something that necessarily sparks my interest—and it usually doesn't since what catches my interest seldom catches other people's and vice versa—I tuck it away. Because I never know when it might give me an idea of something I need for a book I'm writing based on one of the fragments of news or research that did catch my interest.

Combine ideas from your notebooks and idea file. Read over both when you're plotting a new book and let them soak into your subconscious. You never know what bit of this or piece of that will become a vital part of your storyline in some intriguing way. Let your active plotting, your notes, and your idea file build on one another as you're creating characters, situations, motivations, and actions for your story. Maybe the combination of two or three of these ideas and notes together will offer the complexity you need.

Start right away with two documents—a list of questions about the characters, locations, situation, and story/plot actions to which you'll add constantly at the beginning and a first-draft journal or a document of first-draft notes. These can be written by hand in a notebook or in a computer document. The important thing is to have these documents or something very like them and to write in them, thinking on paper about your fictional place, people, and plot. Another useful document I've discovered is a list of scenes you want to see or write in the book—at the very beginning of the process before you really know what else will happen. In the sample documents at the end of the book, you will find copies of these three documents that I used in writing one of my own novels, and we will discuss ways in which you can use your own versions of these documents.

Journal or Notes

Begin a first-draft journal by hand or on the computer or else a document of first-draft notes, things you want to remind yourself to do, research, or think about regarding the book. The important thing is to have these documents or something very like them and to write in them often, thinking on paper about your fictional place, people, and plot. (See Sample of First Draft Journal Document and Sample of First Draft Notes Document.)

These are where you will find your book taking shape and, consequently, are important to your book. You will want a place to keep all your important thoughts, random thoughts, and the results of your thinking on paper about your book to consult again and again as you plan, write, and revise your novel.

Exercise 1: Begin by writing the opening pages of your own journal or notes for this exercise. This is a way of talking to yourself on paper and working out what you know, what you don't know but will need to figure out, what you want to do in the book, what problems you see arising, and possible ways to solve those problems. Ask yourself questions and respond on paper. Find out what you already know about this book deep inside yourself.

Beginning with Questions

Next, you will want to start an ongoing list of questions to yourself about the characters (especially your protagonist and antagonist), locations, situation, and the story/plot actions. This is a list to which you'll add constantly.

Ask yourself what the initial situation of your characters will be. Ask how this situation came to be. Ask why this will be important and what will trigger the crisis or change that sets the whole story in motion.

Ask yourself where this is all taking place or going to take place. Ask yourself all kinds of questions about these possible locations—about architecture, transportation, government, about the animals that live there, the plants that grow there, the weather and its effect on animals and humans. Ask yourself about the culture of the place and about the emotional atmosphere.

Ask yourself who your protagonist and main characters are and why they get involved in this situation. Ask about their relationships to each other and to the other people in their lives, such as family and friends.

Ask every question you can think of, and then, as you work out the situation, location, and characters while you write, the answers will help write your book.

As you move through planning and plotting the book, you will answer many of these questions in the planning/plotting stages, decide that a few don't matter, and answer the others in the actual writing process. This is an important beginning step to plotting a novel.

Exercise 2: For this exercise, set down at least ten questions to start yourself off. (See the document Beginning Questions for *Every Broken Trust* for examples.)

Thinking About Scenes

Scenes are the building blocks of story and plot. A scene usually takes place in one location only, though occasionally a scene may move from room to room or from indoors to outside in the course of one scene. That usually happens when a continuing dialogue or action takes place while the characters move from room to room or from inside to outdoors during the conversation or action. In a scene, the focus in close while the reader watches and hears what is actually said and done. In other words, it is shown to the reader and fully dramatized.

If it is merely told, it would not be a scene but rather a transition, as in "The next morning, he visited his sister's doctor to learn the truth before seeking out Julian for a confrontation." And then we are in a scene at Julian's house with the two of them arguing over the sister and her treatment.

A transitional narrative can cover more than a morning, of course. One such might tell in a few paragraphs of the character's visit to the doctor and then to the sister, who refuses to leave the man who is mistreating her, and then of the situation growing worse over the months until he receives a call that his sister is in the hospital. At this point, months after the last scene, the character may step into a scene at the hospital with the sister where we hear what they say to each other and see how they react to each other, or the character may rush off in fiery anger to burst in on the drunken Julian and threaten him in another fully realized scene.

A novel is a series of scenes that build upon past scenes and connect. The scenes must connect to each other and build upon each other, at least implying causality, for the whole series to constitute a plot or story. I will often refer to that line of causality that runs through the series of scenes as the narrative through-line. This is the most foundational element of narrative structure. Each scene should build off the scene before it or an earlier scene in the book.

I like to think of each scene as a mini-story with the same basic structure—hook, development, climax. The difference between a scene and a full story is that the climax at the end of the scene is not the end. It should show the consequence and result of what has gone before in the scene, but this climax should not be satisfying for your character and should send the character off into the next scene, instead of ending the whole process.

Conflict, large and small, is the key to a good book and a good scene. Make sure something is at stake in each scene, and set up obstacles to your character gaining or saving or achieving what she wants. You will set up what's at stake in the scene during the hook at its beginning. As the scene plays through its development stage, your character is working to achieve what he wants. Even if he does, in the climax of the scene, he must find that something even more important is now threatened, and usually, he will not achieve what he wants in the scene, at least not completely, so he will have to head into the next scene with the same or a new goal. This chain of actions will lead the character to the point where things look hopeless, but she will try one more effort in the climactic scene of the book where she will prevail in one way or another. Scenes are the way you must think of what's going on or what is to happen in your book.

Exercise 1: Another useful document I've discovered in the past few books is a list of scenes you want to see or write in the book—at the very beginning of the process before you really know what else will happen. (See document, Scenes I Want to See in *Every Hidden Fear*. This document has already had the too over-the-top or unbelievable scenes removed, so it looks more controlled than the initial list was or your initial list will be.)

Use the timed freewriting technique to list as many possible scenes for the book as you can. Don't worry if some are wacky or over-the-top. Just keep listing more scenes. Do this several times as you work through the book. You can even do a special list just for the dreaded, flat middle. Later, you can decide some are too flashy or wild or whatever, but by not censoring yourself, you'll come up with a list of strong scenes that you can weave into you narrative, and each of them will suggest one or more scenes before and after, as well.

For this exercise, come up with at least ten scenes you know you want to see in your book, even if you don't know how you'd manage them.

Brainstorming Plot

Brainstorming is a procedure almost everyone knows. It's used in corporate settings, and governmental entities, nonprofits, community organizations, classrooms, and informal gatherings of friends also use it. It can be used in almost any group setting to come up with new and creative solutions to problems.

I like to use it as an individual, however. It's another way to tap into your creative unconscious. Write your topic or question at the top of the sheet of paper or document screen. Set a timer for at least ten minutes—longer is better. (Sometimes, I don't set the timer, but instead set myself a number goal of how many ideas to write down, and I can't stop until I reach that number.) Now, start listing ideas for that topic. Nothing can be rejected. Just keep your pen or fingers on the keyboard moving. Some ideas may be too exotic, impractical, or over-the-top, but just write them down and keep going.

When using this technique for plotting, the best way is to start thinking of the major events of the story. Some of them you may not know—and that's okay. You just skip over them and keep going. Put down every possible event for your book that you can come up with.

Don't worry about order. If some event you come up with for the end of the book makes you think of an event that would be great up at the beginning, just write it down, and keep going. When your time is up or you've reached your desired number of ideas, you can go back and re-order the plot events you created. You can decide to cut out the weird group striptease idea for your cozy mystery or sweet romance as unsuitable, but simply writing it down may well trigger two or three much more usable ideas.

I use this technique also when I'm struggling with problems in writing or revising the novel. Before I set my timer, I pull out my plot outline or scene analysis or whatever format I've put my plot organization in. I read it over, circling or otherwise marking problem areas—plot holes, illogical actions, weak and flabby areas, places where I know my plot's not good but I don't really know why. Then, I set the timer and begin brainstorming. This technique has saved me several times when I was in a real bind.

Brainstorming by yourself has multiple uses. Put it in your novelist's toolbox, and use it often.

Exercise 1: Write your own plot document, starting from the beginning if you're starting a new project or picking up where you are with an ongoing project and filling plot holes or deepening a shallow plot section. Freewrite or use brainstorming techniques of listing rapid-fire questions or suggestions without judgment until your listing time is finished and you can go back and decide which have value for you alone or in combination with others, and which don't. (See Sample of Freewriting Plot Document.)

You will notice some overlap with the journal and notes here. Often, I will start a session of heavy plot brainstorming/freewriting by copying passages from the journal or notes document that have ideas or things I want to keep in mind. This can work as a kind of priming-the-pump for the mind in coming up with ideas.

Thinking About Protagonists

Even if you begin with an intriguing location or a dramatic situation, you will soon need to start developing a protagonist to deal with both. The protagonist is a major component of your novel, if not the major component. If you think of all the great books you've read, how many plots or backgrounds spring to mind? Isn't it usually the characters that keep that novel alive in your memory?

Every novel needs to give the reader a character who will be the lens through which the reader will view the story, even if there are other viewpoint characters. This is the character the reader will care about, root for, worry about, want to know what's going to happen to her/him next or what s/he's going to do next. The reader may not like this character, but the reader wants to see what's going to happen next in this character's story. The reader is supremely interested and invested in this character.

So, how do we go about creating this character? We develop her by digging deeply into her emotional makeup. We learn him through his most basic emotions—desire, fear—and his obsessions.

Look at your protagonist's greatest fears and desires. In this process, pay attention to fears and desires, above all, for out of those emotions come other motives like hate, jealousy, greed, anger, deceit, and so many others. Ask yourself <u>on paper</u> what crime or challenge this character could face that would draw on those basic emotions of fear or desire. We always want to make the struggle for high stakes—a love that will leave your character empty and aching if he loses it, custody of her beloved child, a promotion that will signal to your character's father that he's finally a success. In most mysteries or thrillers, that might seem easy because the crime involved is almost always murder, but how can you make that even worse and more personal for your protagonist?

I have stressed so heavily that you do this in writing because it is too easy to believe we are thinking our way through something, only to find, when we have to write that scene or book, that we were really sort of daydreaming about it. Writing is thinking on paper. The very act of writing out our questions and thoughts leads us to answers and new possibilities. The very act of writing changes your brain. It moves you into creative problem-solving mode.

We will use the answers derived from this freewriting to outline a plot driven by the protagonist's motivation and interaction with the world. We always want to begin with a character on the brink of some action because that provides a lot of forward momentum. Then we want to put that protagonist through hell as s/he tries to reach a desired goal. The reader will stay with you in suspense if you make it real because everything that happens is rooted in your character's motivations as they conflict with other characters and the external environment and with their own fears and obsessions.

Exercise 1: Set your timer for at least 10 minutes, preferably 20 or more, for each question and freewrite.

A) What are my character's greatest desires?

B) What are my character's greatest fears?

C) What crime or challenge could this character face that would draw on those basic emotions of fear or desire?

Creating a Protagonist Readers Will Invest in Emotionally

Freewriting is the technique that I've found most helpful for this kind of deep character work. You may be familiar with it from one of the many writing teachers who teach it now, each calling it something different such as Morning Pages or timed writing. Or you may less commonly know it from the woman who first started it, Dorothea Brande, or the great writing teacher and novelist, John Gardner, who brought her work back to the attention of writers in the second half of the 20th century (including all those who now teach it as their own). And of course, you've had a chance to try it out in short sprints in earlier lessons, but now we'll be doing longer, deeper sessions.

For this freewriting, you set a timer for twenty or more minutes and write about the set topic without stopping until the timer goes off. This allows your brain to pour out all the shallow conscious stuff you're aware of on that topic and then to dig into the riches your unconscious has learned or created on the same subject. For characters, I do this in first person from their viewpoint, as if they were writing their own diary. When beginning a character, I just write generally from that character's viewpoint, but later when trying to understand motivation, I will give a question to write about, such as "Why did you kill Jake?" I have found that the longer I set my timer for, the deeper I go and the more really rich and complex a character I start to develop.

In the last section, you took a surface look at your protagonist's fears, desires, secrets, and weaknesses. Now, we're trying to go deeper into that character, so write longer, going deeper about your character's obsessions, dreams, terrors.

You want to know all you can about these emotions and their triggers for this character, because you will use them later to motivate that character to do things for good or evil. If you try to move characters around a predetermined plot like paper dolls or puppets, you will find your book less than successful. If every decision and action your characters take is fully motivated and you and the reader know why s/he's making and taking them, your book will engage your reader, and the narrative drive will pull him or her along to keep turning pages.

Next, ask why your character's friends love her/him. Try freewriting from two or three different friends' points of view. Then, write a conversation between two friends about your character. This allows you to see your characters as other characters view them, both positively and negatively. I guarantee that, if you do this right, you will surprise yourself with what you will learn about your characters.

Finally, look at the character's name, his/her physical description, and descriptive tags and mannerisms. These will all play into or against the traits your character has already developed. I deliberately hold off until this stage of character development to decide on the character's name because names are so powerful that choosing a name can limit or distort the character's development. So much unconscious expectation and baggage goes along with the name that I've found it better to wait until the character is starting to shape up, and then to choose a name based on the character that has already begun to form.

And one final tip, let's not make them models or actors or superheroes, please. It can get very boring reading about women who could be cover girls or starlets and men who could give Brad Pitt or George Clooney a run for their money. No one will buy it if your character has so much strength, skill, speed, and invulnerability that s/he should be wearing spandex and a cape. The idea is to make your character a real person who lives and breathes on the page, not a comic-book hero or villain.

It's at this stage that I sometimes begin to keep a writing notebook for the book. I have sections for Title Ideas, Chronology, Initial Situation, Theme, Background/Setting, Characters, Development, Outline, Questions, and Research, but you might find some others more helpful. This idea came from Phyllis Whitney, a writer of children's mysteries and romantic suspense novels. I used it originally by handwriting in a three-ring notebook. I tried to transfer it to the computer and never quite made it work for me there, so I began to take different sections and make them into separate documents. If you use Scrivener or yWriter or some other novel-writing program, you probably already have something similar on the computer. I offer it for those who might find it useful. (I'm about to start work on a new series, and I think I'll set up a three-ring notebook like this again and do the initial work in there.)

Exercise 2: Freewrite for at least 20 minutes in your protagonist's first-person viewpoint (as if s/he was talking to a trusted friend or writing a diary entry), exploring in greater depth her/his fears, desires, secrets, weaknesses, and obsessions. Remember the trick is to keep the pen or cursor moving, even if you must write the last word over and over until more comes. You are trying to short-circuit your conscious mind and tap into the unconscious. If you're lucky, you will begin to write in your character's voice. It may take you two or three times of trying this freewriting in the character's voice before it starts to work for you, Don't despair. Be patient. If you keep trying, it will come, and you'll find the character's voice taking form on the page. Don't overthink—that's the enemy of this exercise. Just write whatever comes.

Exercise 3: Next, try freewriting from two or three different friends' points of view, and ask why your character's friends love her/him. Do at least 10 minutes freewriting for each friend.

Exercise 4: Write an honest conversation between two of those friends about your protagonist, perhaps one where the friends are concerned about her/him. This allows you to see your characters as other characters view them, both positively and negatively.

Thinking about Villains

Students often ask me whether one should have sympathetic murderers or not. This is a perennial question in crime writing. There are no right or wrong answers. Each of us may come to different conclusions for our own work, but at least, we should think seriously about the issue and make our decisions consciously.

Some people feel that the only way they can justify the violence, explicit or implied (in cozies), in crime writing is to make the perpetrators unsympathetic and punish them heavily. They see this as a moral decision.

I understand their position, but it's not my own. Some of my murderers are unpleasant people, greedy and selfish. Some of my murderers are pleasant, kind people, who have allowed their emotions to highjack their ethics—sometimes in a moment of rage or jealousy—and then slid further down the slope of evil actions as they tried to cover up what they had done.

I want my antagonists to be fully human, and that is what I suggest you do, as well. If you want to always make your murderer unsympathetic, that's fine, but make him believably human while you're at it. Create a real person, who happens to be unsympathetic.

We've seen how important the protagonist's character is to reader suspense. He or she has to be earning the reader's backing. But the antagonist's character is just as important for true suspense. Every novel will have at least one antagonist, even if it's not a crime novel. Someone wants the love affair to fail for some reason and works toward that end. Someone else wants that promotion and is working hard to get it.

The ex-spouse or a grandparent is trying to win custody of that beloved child. There can only be one winner of the contest or pageant, but there are six or twelve contestants. Your protagonist desperately wants something, and someone stands in the way.

The antagonist must be worthy of the hero, however, and capable of providing clever and devilish problems for the hero that will really stretch the protagonist. You have to fully develop her or him. No Snidely Whiplashes allowed. *Just because he's evil* is not a character motivation. Neither is *just because she's crazy*. The mentally ill are much more likely to be the victims of violence and malice than the perpetrators. Evil and Crazy are signs of a lazy writer.

Unless you're doing first-person narration by the protagonist, allow the reader to know the antagonist's motivation and make it strong, so the reader will understand why he takes the stand he does and will believe that he's dedicated to what he's doing to undermine or destroy the protagonist. If your story is a first-person protagonist narrative, once again you can attempt to let the reader know the antagonist's motivation through dialogue overheard or another character telling the protagonist or some other bit of news that will tell the reader why the antagonist is determined and just how very determined he is.

I also think it's important to remember that everyone is the hero of her/his own story. The villain never sees herself as the villain, but as the hero, righting wrongs or getting what she deserves in the only way she can or protecting herself or others or her reputation, etc. If you've ever worked or taught in the justice system, you know that criminals always think it was everyone else's fault and they only did what they had to do.

So when creating your antagonist, remember this. Think

of villains that have fan followings, such as Hannibal Lector or Dexter the serial killer of graphic novel and TV series fame. Everyone knows what they do is horrible, but their authors have shown their motivations and made them real, likable people. I'm not a big fan of creating a monstrous villain that people will really, really like—at least, it's not something I personally want to do—but we can learn from these examples that giving our antagonists real motivations and good qualities can make them more believable.

Using Character as a Springboard to a Strong Plot

A strong, vibrant plot is one of the elements of a great novel, along with complex, living characters and great writing. Oddly enough, work on creating a strong, vibrant plot and complex, living characters often goes on at the same time. Each major aspect of your novel cross-fertilizes the other in a symbiotic relationship.

Start with your character's greatest fear, desire, and obsession. Use the first-person character freewriting we practiced earlier to learn what they are.

Next, bring that fear into the story. Force your character to face it. If he or someone he loves is in danger, let the only hope of rescue be through the worst fear the character has, whether it is fire, heights, enclosed spaces, or snakes (think Indiana Jones).

Thwart the desire in a major way. Use physical injury, mechanical failures, natural disasters, betrayal by allies, the petty obstacles of daily life (like traffic jams), and any other kind of obstacle or rejection you can.

Use the obsession to cause your character to make bad decisions or faulty judgments. Allow it to blind her to the people and things which might help her and believe in those people and institutions which will hinder or betray her. Let it send her in the wrong direction and lead her to choices that will cause delay or damage.

Answer the question, "How can you make things bad and then worse for your character?" We all like our protagonists and sidekicks, but as authors we need to treat them as if we hate them. If we allow everything to work out easily for them and give them no actual struggle, we have a boring story. This is one of the problems with protagonists who are ultra-beautiful, -handsome, -strong, -skilled, etc. They have no need to struggle, and there's never any doubt that they will triumph. A little weakness, a major personality flaw, a phobia that must be faced, a want he can't fulfill, a dream out of reach, all of these help to make a story exciting.

Make the struggle your character must go through important. It must be for high stakes. A mystery's stakes usually have to be solving a murder and finding justice for the victim, of course, but how can you make it even worse? Could someone else, especially someone close to the protagonist, be under threat from the murderer? Could the protagonist's spouse/lover/family member/friend/business partner be suspected of or charged with the murder? Could the protagonist herself be suspected/charged? Could a beloved institution or a long-desired business success be threatened by the unsolved murder?

If you're not writing a mystery, try to find ways to heighten the stakes for your character. Every protagonist has to have a goal s/he's trying to achieve. Put obstacles, large and small, in the way, and deepen the consequences of failure. Perhaps if your character can't get this last-chance job, she could lose her home or custody of her children or her parents' approval or her paroled status. Find some way to raise the stakes.

Ask yourself how your character's flaws and vulnerabilities can make things worse for him. If he's mouthy, does he spoil the chance to get information or help he desperately needed because he was too sarcastic, flip, and insulting to the wrong person? If she's stubborn, does she refuse to listen to good advice from a friend or mentor? If he fears heights, can the information or proof he needs or the rescue of someone in danger only be won by a struggle at the top of a skyscraper or

high cliff? If she fears enclosed spaces, can she only escape
the killer's attempts on her life by crawling through a long
tunnel or deep into a cave?

Allow your character to fail or make the wrong decision
because of one of his weaknesses. Let his prejudice for or
against someone blind him to their real nature and drop him
into serious trouble. Let her anger problems cause her to
shout out something to the wrong person in an argument
that allows the killer to know she's on to him and needs to
be disposed of or offends the person who makes the ultimate
decision as to whether she gets that shot at stardom or not.
Allow him to initially accuse the wrong person or act out
in the wrong circumstances because of his impulsive nature.
Then, write the scene where your character realizes what s/
he's done, where s/he is faced with the consequences.

Ask yourself what would stretch your character's strengths
and virtues to the limit and beyond. Our job as writers is
to put our characters into situations where they are forced
to grow and develop. Give your protagonist a true test of
character, one where something he wants conflicts with
another thing he wants or where one thing she fears conflicts
with another thing she desires.

Give your protagonist real trouble and then triple it. Let
her professional ambition be threatened, and at the same
time, throw her best friend in danger while tossing in the
potential for financial or social-reputation disaster. On top
of that, send every daily-life difficulty her way—cell phones
with dead batteries, cars that won't start, tire blowouts, traffic
jams, late trains or buses, streets closed for construction, lost
keys, computer hard drives that crash, etc.

Add a kid, a pet, a best friend, or a love interest in danger.
This has to be very real danger—of physical damage, death,
arrest, severe psychological damage, destruction of some

hope that's vital to your character. It can't be trivial. Then, set things up so that the only way your protagonist can save that kid/friend is by doing what he fears or hates most or by losing what he most wants in this world. Think real sacrifice when you're writing this part. Remember, this needs to be a true test of her character.

At the end of this book, you will find a sample of a freewriting character document I usually write for every major character and a sample of a plotting and brainstorming document. Combined with the character work, this kind of weaving back and forth between deepening character and using what you learn there to make the plot more complex and exciting is something that goes on throughout the writing of the book.

Exercise 1: Answer these questions in a timed freewriting session for each question. This time, put the whole thing in first person narration. Write as if you were the protagonist talking or writing a journal entry. (See Sample Character Freewriting document.)

A. What does your protagonist most want/desire/need in this book?

B. How does the situation in which s/he finds her/himself impact this?

C. Why does s/he say s/he has this want/need?

D. What is the real reason, possibly a secret from her/himself?

E. What/who does your protagonist most fear/hate/envy in this book?

F. Who has hurt/shamed/rejected her/him in the past and how does that affect her/him now?

G. What is the secret(s) your protagonist keeps even from her/himself? What are her/his weaknesses and vulnerabilities?

Develop Suspense and Anticipation

Every novel needs suspense elements to keep the reader turning the page. At its simplest, suspense consists of making the reader want to know what happens next. At its best, suspense is making the reader worry that his beloved protagonist will never reach his overpowering need or goal... and what on earth is going to happen next? You will find this kind of suspense in all kinds of good novels. Will Atticus Finch be able to save innocent Tom Robinson's life in *To Kill a Mockingbird*? Will Scarlett O'Hara save Tara in *Gone with the Wind*? Will Paul Atreides be able to become the Kwisatz Haderach to defeat the evil Harkonnens and the Emperor in *Dune*? There are a number of ways to provide suspense in a story. I say "provide" rather than "insert" because the suspense needs to be integral to the story and not just something added on.

One of the most important ways to increase suspense is to make it clear to the reader at the beginning of the story just what is at stake. It must be something that threatens to devastate the protagonist's self-image, life or world, and he must be willing to make any sacrifice and go to any lengths to keep this from happening. However, another fine way to keep the reader wanting to know what happens next is to open your story or book deep in the action and explain it later. Although these strategies seem contradictory, they can be combined to add powerful elements of tension and apprehension to the reader's experience of the book. If you start in the middle of some strong action scene, and then in the next scene or chapter, establish the background of your characters and the situation, you can delineate the high stakes that are involved for your protagonist here. These combined strategies can be used in almost any kind of story.

An alternative to this kind of two-part opening can be a first scene or chapter that establishes the protagonist within her everyday world but buries hints of impending change or danger within these ordinary moments. This is foreshadowing, and it has been misused often, but when the hints are subtle enough (while still being apparent to the attentive reader), foreshadowing can build excellent suspense. Movies have it easier here because they can use the background music to warn the audience that something wicked this way comes. Writers must try to create that same kind of atmosphere with sharp dissonant details and atmosphere.

One of the key ways to ensure that your book has the kind of suspense that keeps the reader saying, "Just one more page," is to offer the reader the viewpoints of both the protagonist and the antagonist. This way the reader can see the problems the antagonist is planning for the protagonist long before the protagonist is aware of them. The reader can see what the protagonist cannot—that he's on a collision course with disaster. This is a very powerful tool for suspense in all genres of novels, but is unavailable to those of you with a first-person protagonist-only viewpoint.

In the case of the first-person protagonist viewpoint, you can avail yourself of some of that reader foresight of disaster with the traditional tricks of the mystery writer. In the traditional mystery, as opposed to the suspense novel or thriller, the reader is in the dark and trying to figure out what happened and who the villain is at the same time as the protagonist does. Write in details that plant questions in the reader's mind about the various characters, their secrets and motivations, about what really happened in the past, especially with a murder, and about what might happen in the future through clues and red herrings. Clues are actual evidence of what has happened or might happen, while red herrings are false harbingers, leading the protagonist and the reader in the wrong direction. Either of these can increase the reader's need to know what's going to happen and can be used to heighten suspense in all novels, not just mysteries.

All characters have some secrets, even from themselves. Something that reveals one of these secrets, perhaps one that someone has lied about, will build suspense. When using clues and red herrings to increase suspense, keep the ratio of clues to red herrings high in the favor of real clues to keep from annoying the reader.

Another way to use clues is to plant some detail that brings uneasiness but is made to seem innocuous at the time. Later, this detail will turn out to be an important harbinger of some violence or problem. This stems from Chekhov's gun on the wall which must go off before the play is over, or Brian Garfield's famous dictum—"Plant it early. Pay it off later."

A great technique to ratchet up tension in a book or story is to use a deadline. Time becomes the enemy and is working for the villain in this technique. The bomb is ticking, and our heroine must find it and disarm it while that clock on it is inexorably ticking down to explosion and other obstacles are thrown in her way inevitably slowing her down. It needn't be an actual clock or bomb, and it needn't be minutes counting down to disaster. It could be months or years if we've been given a large enough view and long enough timeline at the beginning of the book, although most traditional mysteries or suspense/thrillers will use a more compressed timeline. Again, this is a technique that can be used with any novel.

Suspense is always present when the reader knows the protagonist is fighting seemingly overwhelming odds. The reader wants to see him stretched to the breaking point as he tries to prevent the feared disaster (remembering that this is a disaster in the protagonist's eyes, not necessarily a "blow-up-the-world" disaster). Your character must learn new skills, access new abilities, overcome old flaws in ways he never thought he could in order to save the day. This kind of determination will keep the reader turning pages to find out what happens to him next.

We've seen how important the protagonist's character is to reader suspense. He or she has to be earning the reader's backing. But the antagonist's character is just as important for true suspense. The antagonist must be worthy of the hero and capable of providing clever and devilish problems for the hero that will really stretch the protagonist. Unless you're doing first-person narration by the protagonist, allow the reader to know the antagonist's motivation and make it strong, so the reader will believe that he's dedicated to what he's doing to undermine or destroy the protagonist. If your story is a first-person protagonist narrative, once again you can attempt to let the reader know the villain's motivation through dialogue overheard or another character telling the protagonist about it or some other bit of news that will tell the reader why the antagonist is determined and just how very determined he is.

An important but often overlooked way to ratchet up tension and suspense is to allow daily life to throw extra obstacles in the protagonist's way. She's trying to get to the old house where her child's been left by the bad guy before the flood waters drown the kid, but it's rush hour and there's a huge accident and traffic jam, or she runs out of gas on the deserted creepy road to the house, or the flood waters have brought out alligators or poisonous snakes, or the street she needs to take has been blocked off for road repairs, or her ratty old car that she can't afford to replace refuses to start, or... None of these are things the antagonist did, but they impede her nonetheless. This technique also has the positive effect of increasing reader identification with the hero. The reader knows what it is to be in a hurry to get somewhere important and encounter a traffic jam or blocked-off road. It also helps with the writer's most important goal—verisimilitude. We all want to make our story-world become so real to the reader that he will never wake from the story-dream.

These are just a few of the best ways to use suspense to keep your reader engaged. Suspense is a technique every writer can use. It's a matter of creating a steam engine with no whistle, so that the steam builds in pressure, and at any time there could be an explosion. As a writer, in a thousand ways, great and small, your job is to keep turning up the heat under that engine.

In my own mystery-suspense novel, *Every Last Secret*, I can show some of these techniques right in the jacket copy. I'll bold them.

Marquitta "Skeet" Bannion fled a big-city police force and painful family entanglements for the **peace of a small Missouri college town** and a job as chief of campus police. Now, the **on-campus murder** of the student newspaper editor who **traded in secrets** puts Skeet on the trail of **a killer who will do anything to keep a dangerous secret from being exposed.** While Skeet struggles to **catch a murderer and prevent more deaths,** a **vulnerable boy and ailing father** tangle family responsibilities around her once again. **Time is running out** and **college administrators demand she sweep all college involvement under the rug,** but **Skeet won't stop** until she's unraveled every last secret.

Do you see? Secrets, high stakes, motivated and strong antagonist, overwhelming obstacles, everyday difficulties, a deadline, and dedicated protagonist.

Exercise 1: Writing a jacket summary or short synopsis of your book can be a valuable tool as you progress. Without giving away anything, summarize the key points of your story in one or two paragraphs. So write one for your own book.

(NOTE: It's not at all easy to do this well and takes a long time to get it right usually, but when you finally have it done well, you have something you can use with agents, editors, and on the back cover of your book.)

Next, take your book's synopsis/summary and try bolding or underlining all the various techniques of suspense you find in yours. If you only find one or two, you'll want to rethink your story so it will include more elements of suspense to keep your readers turning the page.

Challenge Your Character

Look at your protagonist's deepest emotions for possibilities of situations that can stretch your protagonist to the limit and provide great suspense. In this process, pay attention to fears and desires above all, for out of those emotions come other motives like hate, jealousy, greed, anger, deceit, and so many others. Ask yourself *on paper* what crime or challenge this character could face that would draw on those basic emotions of fear or desire. We always want to make the struggle for high stakes. In most mysteries or thrillers, the crime involved has to be murder but how can you make it worse?

I have stressed so heavily that you do this in writing because it is too easy to believe we are thinking our way through something, only to find, when we have to write that scene or book, that we were really sort of daydreaming about it. Writing is thinking on paper. The very act of writing out our questions and thoughts leads us to answers and new possibilities. The act of writing it out and thinking on paper helps us to see which thoughts are useful and lead toward resolution of the problem and which are not. Always do your thinking about your book on paper, and you will find possibilities and answers to which you wouldn't otherwise have access.

So make a listing of all the possible ways you can leverage your character's emotions to create greater suspense. Set your timer for 15+ minutes and keep that pen/cursor moving without any editing or censorship. You are trying to outrun the conscious mind with its need for control and come up with rich ways to craft suspense. Some of your list may be too over-the-top or unbelievable, but that doesn't matter. Just keep going until your alarm goes off. The longer you can manage, the deeper you will go and the better your list will be. Later, you can select all the best items for your plot.

Exercise 1: Set your timer for 15+ minutes, and brainstorm all the possible ways you can leverage your character's fears, desires, and obsessions to create heart-stopping (or at least, page-turning) suspense.

Complicate the Plot Through Secondary Characters

A protagonist alone does not a novel make, nor does a book with only a protagonist and an antagonist. There have been a few very unusual books with only the two characters, but in general, we need more than those two main actors to have a story that will keep people engaged to the very end.

How do we come up with good secondary characters and meanwhile flesh out even more those major two, the protagonist and antagonist? We will use the tools we've already been using in building character—freewriting, brainstorming on paper, and listing questions to answer. And once we've built a world full of individual people among whom our protagonists will exist and interact, we will start to bring some order to it to make it easier to write—and to figure out when and where we've gone off track.

But we'll deal with that in our exercise later. Right now, let's consider the importance of secondary characters—from major ones like best friends or love interests to minor ones like the stubborn bureaucrat with the vital bit of information the protagonist needs.

What will your characters tell you, if given the chance?

First of all, your characters, major and minor, will tell you how to make them do the things they fear or hate most in the world. Remember, in order to have the kind of high stakes that make readers worry about our characters and keep turning the pages, we must make it necessary for them to face that debilitating fear or dreaded thing/person. If we let them, our characters will tell us not only what those fears and hates are, but how to force them to deal with them at the most extreme. Your characters, if you work with them on paper, will tell you what each character's lever is, the emotion/event/situation that will push that character to the wall and make him do things he would ordinarily never do.

Secondly, this kind of deep character work on paper will tell you why your antagonist is doing these terrible things. We must always remember to make him/her a real person with real needs, wants, and fears. Freewrite to know him better, to understand his lever, what drove/drives her to do the things she does. Remember, antagonists don't think they're evil. Like everyone, they are the heroes of their own stories. If anything, she thinks it's everyone/someone else's fault—he made her do it. So you must find a way to let the reader know why she's doing all these things. Don't make it because he's *evil*. We don't need any Snidely Whiplashes. They only bore readers. Also, mentally ill does not equal *evil*. When we writers use mental illness as an excuse for severely harmful actions of an antagonist, including murder, we are taking the lazy, easy way out. Statistics show that mentally ill people are vastly more likely to be subjected to the violence of others than to commit violence themselves.

Thirdly, this character work will tell you why other members of your cast might want to impede, hurt, or kill the victim and others. This is especially important in mysteries or thrillers because you need suspects. Otherwise the reader knows the antagonist is the one responsible for everything. Other characters need valid motives to harm the victim and any others who are threatened, motives that the reader will really believe.

This kind of deep analysis of your characters can also show you how to change one antagonist for another. I have stopped in the middle of a book, realizing that the murderer I intended was simply too obvious. I turned to character brainstorming and freewriting on secondary characters, hoping to create stronger suspects so the reader wouldn't automatically leap to the correct conclusion. In the process, however, I discovered someone else, never intended as the murderer, who made a much better, more complex murderer than the one originally intended, making for a much stronger book.

Fourthly, character work like this can show you how your protagonist can use his or her flaw or weakness to get out of danger. You can't always do this, but when you can, it makes for such a satisfying experience for the reader that it's best to try for it whenever you have the chanc. If you can make the very flaw that the protagonist has been worrying about and battling against all book become the actual tool he needs to save himself and others or solve the crime, the reader will reward you for it with loyalty to your books. One of my favorite examples of this occurred in Nancy Pickard's first mystery novel, *Generous Death*. Her protagonist has been plagued by lack of confidence, since she's a woman who runs a nonprofit foundation (in what was then a man's world) and hasn't the skills, weapons, or strength a police officer would have to defeat a stronger adversary. In the climax, she's alone, cut off from all help with no weapon, so she turns her bra, that common aspect of womanhood, into a weapon and strangles the killer with it when he tries to murder her.

Brainstorm as many ways out of that final climactic scene of jeopardy as you can find, and choose the best. Be sure to make it a real struggle, not just ignorance on the antagonist's part, that wins out for your protagonist.

Finally, working all this out on paper will tell you why other characters will help or hinder your character's quest. In Daniel Woodrell's classic novel, *Winter's Bone*, even the protagonist's relatives put up obstacles and try to stop her search for her father. Yet unlikely characters turn helpful. Your other characters are there to inform, mislead, or otherwise help or try to stop your protagonist's search for answers and justice. When a friend or ally turns on the character, it's a strong emotional kick. In *Winter's Bone*, one of the most powerful moments comes when the women who have had real sympathy for the protagonist (who's a young girl) turn on her. Betrayal (or seeming betrayal) always packs a tremendous wallop and leaves the reader reeling if he trusted that character the same way your protagonist did.

Exercise 1: Using one or more of the methods learned in previous chapters—character freewriting, brainstorming on paper, listing questions—develop at least one secondary character as a suspect. Find a strong motivation and ways to display it in action or substantial clues that would make a reader think this character could be the culprit the protagonist is seeking. You only need to do one character for this exercise, but for your book, you will want to do more.

Bonus points if you can figure out a great secret betrayal (or, even better, some act that feels like betrayal but eventually turns out not to be) that will blindside your protagonist and reader.

Naming and Describing Characters

Naming characters is a job every writer of fiction has to do—and most of us dread, to a certain extent. We chat about the vicissitudes of character-naming on Facebook all the time.

"How did I manage to come up with five different major characters whose names all begin with the letter 'D'?"

"Quick! What's a good name for a guy who likes fast cars and risky situations? It can't begin with a 'D,' 'K,' or 'R,' and it can only have one syllable."

For writers who've published a number of books, an extra problem is added to the mix. The name can't be one they've used in a past book for a major character.

How do you find a variety of real-sounding, yet individual names? How do you avoid calling everyone John Smith and Jane Doe?

I collect first and last names, keeping a long, long list on my computer that I can peruse when I need a new character name. I run down these lists looking for a first and last name that click for the personality that character has already built up. I draw these names from telephone books, high school yearbooks, organization membership lists, anthology contributors, the credits of movies, the lists of contributors to events I attend (keep those programs with the long lists of donors!), genealogy sites and records (great sources for historical-period or ethnic names), and just about any other source I can think of. I don't use baby-name lists, although I will use those to look up meanings of names. And even though, my lists cover multiple pages by now, I still add to them whenever I find a good source—or even just a good name.

You want the name to be appropriate to the character's generation because first names definitely go in trends. You want to consider what the name connotes about the character—Salston Cordwainer III versus Sly Marzo. You want the name to be authentic to the ethnic heritage you've given the character—no Chinese last names for Thai characters, please, and I beg of you to forebear what seems the overwhelming need of many white writers to make up an "Indian" name, such as Dancing Elk or Silent-As-The-River.

Also, you want the major character names to begin with different letters and not all sound alike—Sherry, Debby, Sandy, Jerry, Larry, etc. Avoid anything that will confuse your reader or make it difficult for her/him to tell your characters apart.

Develop and Combine Characters for Deeper Reader Involvement

When you've read through your entire first-draft manuscript, you can easily come to one of two conclusions, that there are too many characters in your book—or not enough characters. Actually, the problem you face may well be neither an overdose of characters nor a shortage of them. The real problem is most likely that your characters are not complex and richly developed enough for the reader to be satisfied from his interactions with them. When it comes to shallow, cardboard characters, they will always be too many and yet never enough to provide satisfaction.

Look at your cast of characters and identify which ones are important to your story—protagonist, antagonist, protagonist's friends/family, antagonist's allies, suspects, victims (some of these may be suspects), and characters who contribute key pieces of information/aid or add to the obstructions your protagonist faces.

Begin with these last characters, who can be made into major characters in their own right by playing a key role in a subplot. If one of your major subplot characters is the one who happens to give the key clue or help or to obstruct the protagonist when s/he is closing in on the antagonist, this will tie your subplot even more closely into the main plot and increase its complexity. Every time, you can get rid of a walk-on character, who has to be there only to tell of the missing X, by turning her/him into a major character in a subplot, you win. You can do this by replacing a necessary walk-on with an already important (from subplot) character, or you can do it by combining the necessary qualities of the walk-on with the necessary qualities of a subplot-important character to create a new character who fills both functions.

Now, look at the earlier characters in your list in the same way. Any time you can slot someone who plays one of these roles into one of the others or into a subplot, they're doing double-duty and strengthening the book. Usually, to do this well, you must dig deeper into that character and learn more about him/her. The technique I use for this is that freewriting in the first-person viewpoint of the character that we used earlier.

Story Structure

You can't have story without structure, whether that structure is deliberate or accidental. If there's no structure, there's no story. A random slice of ordinary life, unshaped or unselected, is not a story. A disconnected series of events, no matter how violent or exciting, is not a story. A story has a beginning, a middle, and an end. It has one goal that spans the entire story, along with lesser goals along the way to reaching or resolving that larger goal.

You can think of these as questions—one large one hanging over the entire book and only resolved at the end with smaller and even tiny questions along the way, which are answered as a part of the journey to the big question 's resolution at the end. You never answer a smaller question without raising one or more other small and tiny questions that must be solved in order to reach the resolution of the major question at the end of the book.

Remember, though, that the structure is there to support and move the story. It's seldom rewarding to decide on a structure and force the story and characters into it, whether or not it's a good fit for that story or those characters. When knowledgeable people talk of hack writing, this is what they're talking about (as opposed to those who are ignorant and simply tar every genre book as hack writing regardless of its merits). You will need to design your story structure to fit the kind of story you are writing and to make the best use of your characters and their flaws, vulnerabilities, fears, and desires conflicting with the obsessions, secrets, and passions of other characters.

Stories begin at the moment of change, change that

forces the protagonist(s) to seek to correct something, gain something, or prevent something threatened from happening. Story is the record of that struggle by the protagonist(s) to correct, gain, or save from threat whatever is important to her/him. Succeed, fail, or win at such terrible cost that it hardly feels like a victory, the ending must be earned by the protagonist(s) efforts and sacrifices, leading to growth as a person. Coincidences can never be used to help the protagonist, but will only be believable if they favor the antagonist. The author can never make it easy for her protagonist with, as the ancient Greeks used to call it in their drama, *deus ex machina*, a god introduced onto the stage by a crane at the end to arbitrarily make everything come out right—in other words, just the author rescuing the character and not something the character has earned.

Scenes are the building blocks of structure, and each scene must have its own structure, as if it were a miniature story. It doesn't have to have the same kind of structure as the entire book, and different scenes may take different dramatic structures, but a scene may never be just killing time or providing atmosphere and always must fulfill more than one purpose. Scenes may advance our understanding of one or more characters, provide needed back-story information, bring the setting alive, and many other things, but above and beyond all that, each scene must forward the story, the narrative drive of the book, in some way.

A strong narrative arc will be full of escalation of conflict and tension with at least two reversals (that work against the protagonist's efforts), the last of which should be so serious that the protagonist and the reader should come close to feeling there's no way to overcome this. This is commonly called "the black moment." Only through extraordinary effort does the protagonist overcome this last reversal. (This escalation of conflict and the reversals are where you will use the things revealed to you in all your deep-character work—where s/he will face those greatest fears, be forced to overcome those greatest weaknesses, have to deal with everything s/he's tried to prevent facing in her/his life to this point.)

Many writers, of course, pay no conscious attention to story structure. Most of these writers are unpublished because their stories fail in one way or another (which could, of course, be said about most writers, in general), but a number of writers are quite successful this way. It's not that their stories don't have structure—they do. It's that the writers have internalized the demands of story, perhaps from long, serious reading, perhaps from sheer luck. Most of us need to give it some thought, at least, however.

Exercise 1. Much of finding out or developing your story's structure involves our old technique-friends of freewriting questions and brainstorming lists. Use the following to help you with your own.

1. What problem does the situation present to your protagonist? How can the protagonist eventually resolve that external conflict?

2. List at least five obstacles in the way of your protagonist resolving this conflict. Make at least two of them internal conflicts.

3. How will your protagonist grow because of confronting these obstacles?

4. What do you want to happen at the end of the book?

5. What will have to happen to the protagonist against her/his will to make this end come about?

Begin to Create Order Out of Your Plot

Check out the sample documents at the end of this book, Sample of Chapter Outline and Sample of Scene Analysis. These are two ways of many of beginning to create order out of your plot. Some people also use index cards with scenes on them, whiteboards, mind-mapping programs, or commercial outlining software, standalone or included in a total writing package such as Scrivener or yWriter. Choose one of these two sample methods and work on your plot, using all the insights and ideas gained so far from our earlier work.

The whole point of these two documents—and all the other methods of outlining or planning plot—is to find the right places for all your plot pieces, to become aware of holes in logic, time, or logistics, to make sure each scene contains a beginning question, conflict, resolution of some kind, and a push toward the next scene's question, and to make sure that the scenes and chapters build on each other creating rising tension throughout the book to the climax.

Note: These are samples of actual documents I used in writing a novel, therefore, especially in the Chapter Outline, you will find notations and highlighting that may puzzle you. These were put into the document as I went through the process of writing and revising the book to keep me on track, i.e., number of pages per chapter and scene, etc. You don't need to include these kinds of things in your own version. Simply take the parts that work for you at this stage of your book.

Create an Exciting and Complex Plot

N ow we're coming to one of the most contentious points of plotting and writing a book. Plotters versus pantsers. I'd like to suggest that it doesn't have to be an either or choice, that you may be happiest and most successful by combining the best of both methods.

I have tried pantsing it and usually ended up stuck at some point until I sat down and plotted how to get out of my quicksand. I've tried writing a full, detailed plot outline ahead of time and become frustrated by the way writing the first draft itself changes the outlined story in large and small ways because of the process. I adopted a practice of outlining a few chapters at a time and it worked for me, but I felt guilty and inadequate until I read one day in Elizabeth George's wonderful *Write Away: One Writer's Approach to Fiction and the Writing Life* that she outlined about 50 pages at a time, wrote those pages, then outlined another 50 pages, and on through the end of the book. So I would urge you to give that method a trial if you find the full outline doesn't work for you.

But how do you go about writing a full or partial outline? And how do you pull all the key pieces together?

One way for crime fiction writers is to plan your murder and backstory first. Then, write backward from that. On paper, channel Hercule Poirot in one of those final all-suspects-in-the-library scenes where he explains step-by-step who did it, why, and how they hid it and who else was suspected and why. Once you have that all down, you can refer to it as you outline and write the book. If you know what happened by and to whom and why, you can just write your way toward that ending. And one of the best ways to do this is to freewrite the murder itself from the killer's viewpoint. Often, this alone can give you enough information to be able to go back and outline your beginning and middle.

A second possibility, that is useful for all novelists, is to choose events relative to your concept, theme, or situation and make a list of scenes that you'd like to see or write in this book. Think of things that are exciting or carry lots of energy and drama. For example, when I was doing this with one book, I decided that I wanted to have my protagonist, Skeet Bannion, have to make a dangerous rescue from a car wreck dangling over a flooding river—because of various things this would show about her and other characters involved and because of the sheer drama of the scene. That became one of the most powerful scenes in the book. Remember also that scenes you really want to write, scenes that excite you, will excite the reader. You just have to plan for them and make sure they play an integral role in the story.

While plotting, remember the magic of conflict. Without conflict, no one cares, and no one will keep turning the pages to find out what happens. Try for major or minor conflict of some kind in each scene. Conflict does not have to be fisticuffs and gunfights. It can be a quarrel. It can be a very subtle, competitive one-upmanship cloaked in meticulous politeness. It can be people who love each other but are coming from different viewpoints that never quite mesh. Conflict can be quiet or noisy. It always stems from someone who wants something who can't have it or fears he can't have it.

I founded a novelist's group in my city a number of years ago, and one of the original members who is still with us happens to be the sweetest, kindest person in the world who makes a living writing New Age self-help and inspiration articles. She's a wonderful writer, but she cannot allow herself to write any conflict. She writes up to that point and then has to make everything all right for her characters. As a person, you couldn't do better than to emulate my dear friend. As a novelist, do not be like her. Conflict, large and small, violent and quiet, is the name of the game.

Finally, as you create your plot outline, make your character run a gauntlet of everything s/he fears and hates. List all those things and plan a scene (or more) around each of them.

Be your protagonist's worst enemy as you write & your antagonist's ally. Constantly escalate your character's baptism by fire. We work to create characters we and the readers will identify with and love, but then we have to do what good authors do—be mean to our characters. As you go through this process, remind yourself continually of the mantra: Raise the stakes—make it worse—make it harder.

In the last section, we looked at the sample of the plot outline for *Every Broken Trust*. In this section, I suggest you check out articles on plotting from various writers on the internet. I've given the websites for you below. I've found each of these helpful in various ways. You may or may not.

WARNING: one of these is from Chuck Wendig's great site, to which I also refer you in the next chapter, Muddled Middles. He gives great writing advice, but he's quite profane, so if that bothers you, just give his site a pass. However, it may be the most useful because he has rounded up almost all the methods of plotting. I won't bowdlerize his work or paraphrase it, however. I feel strongly about respecting a writer's own words. So if profanity will bother you, best not to read it.

All of these are to give options about the way to bring a little order to the mass of information on characters, motivation, story, and plot that you're gathering. You don't have to use any one form. You don't have to write out the whole book's plot—or any more than the day's writing to come—before you begin.

Chuck Wendig http://terribleminds.com/ramble/2011/09/14/25-ways-to-plot-plan-and-prep-your-story/

PIXAR http://dragonwritingprompts.blogspot.com/p/pixars-22-rules-to-phenomenal.html

C.J. Cherryh http://cherryh.com/www/craftofwriting.htm

Exercise 2: Using one of these forms or any other (spreadsheets, outline formats, dedicated writing software, index cards, storyboards, timelines, etc.), try to bring some order to a small part of your book so that you would feel more confident trying to write the next scene(s). You may want to try more than one method to see which works best for your own creative process.

Muddled Middles

The middle of the novel is the part that gives a large number of writers the most trouble of anything they write. Novelists moan and gripe to each other on social media about weak or saggy middle they're dealing with. If this is a problem you're having, know that you're not alone. Even award-winning and bestselling authors often find themselves in trouble in the middle of their current novel, either as they write the first draft or as they revise and realize that the middle isn't doing what it needs to do to keep the narrative drive going.

Why are you spinning your tires in the middle of the story? Generally, it's either because you don't have a big enough problem to drive a whole novel or because your main character is just wandering around while the story happens to him/her. Here are some things you can do to tighten the wandering-around-middle.

1. Delete most or all of any chapters that don't have enough tension and change, that don't drive the story forward. Add any essential bits to other chapters. (Save deleted stuff on another file.) Or condense two chapters and combine them into one.

2. Delete or condense scenes that lack tension or don't contribute to the plot or characterization. Condense parts where scenes drag, eliminating the boring bits. (Take out the parts that readers skip over.)

3. Start scenes and chapters later and end them sooner. Cut out the warm-up and cool-down.

4. Skip over transitional times when not much happens. Replace with one or two sentences, like "Three days later."

5.   A boring scene can always be replaced by an interesting one, usually by raising the stakes or upping the tension.

For the story with not enough plot or complication to drive the narrative, I've learned that, if I'm stuck, it's usually because I don't know something I need to know to move the story forward. Figure out what that is through freewriting work on character and plot and just plain hard thinking on paper, and you can unstick even the most stubborn plot.

1.   Whether you use a three-act structure or a four-act structure, all the acts are equally important. You cannot omit the second one or treat it as less crucial than any of the others, because the result will be a sagging middle. So take the time to make Act 2 as gripping as the others. This should be the place where new problems arise. It's the place where the protagonist is forced to abandon his original plan and move in a new direction to meet an added challenge.

2.   Sagging middles especially result when there is no increase in tension as the plot progresses. In the move towards the climax, your characters should face increasingly bigger obstacles and challenges. Things should get more complicated – never less. Characters should have more at stake as events unfold. The emotions should run higher and deeper. And each event should leave the reader more concerned about what will happen next.

3.   Make a brainstorming list of exciting scenes that could happen to boost the middle. These scenes must tie in to the main plot or a subplot in some way. Choose one or two and then make sure you have the necessary scenes leading up to and away from each of these big scenes. Keeping in mind the protagonist's conflicts, and what he/she has to learn, brainstorm a few situations that are sure to force a "learning experience". What kind of event is most likely to cause trouble for this protagonist? In what situation is the

protagonist most likely to try and fail because of the internal problem? Can you outline a series of events showing rising conflict and higher stakes?

4. Think EVENT—actual discrete happenings where the protagonist interacts, makes decisions, confronts an obstacle, investigates, enlists an ally, makes an enemy, gives in to temptation, searches for something missing, breaks the rules... some action that manifests the protagonist's personality and purpose. Don't forget that each event will have consequences that will bring on the next event.

5. A subplot arc can begin in the middle and carry through to tie in at the climax with the main plot at the end, or it can begin early and climax during the middle, tying into the main plot. Or you can pull out one aspect of the major story arc and turn it into its own separate arc that completes by tying back into the major arc and contributing to it, such as Aragorn and the others in the party, once separated from Frodo and Sam, saving Rohan while Frodo goes on with the Ring in *The Lord of the Rings*. The Ring is the major story arc, but Rohan is its own lesser arc that then ties back into the major arc in a big way at Helm's Deep and again later at the final battle.

Any or all of these options may be useful to your own troublesome middle of the book. Experiment with them and see if they don't help you create a stronger, more active middle that becomes an integral part of a more exciting book.

The following link is to a great resource on the web for writing advice, help, and encouragement, a website by writer Chuck Wendig. WARNING: THIS GUY IS VERY PROFANE. I think he's funny. His profanity is wildly creative without being just an onslaught of f-bombs, but I know he could be very upsetting to some people, so if profanity bothers you, do not go to his website. But if that's not a problem, you will find a great deal of helpful stuff here. This link is to his post on middles, again a great round-up of many methods to strengthen your problem middle.

http://terribleminds.com/ramble/2012/06/05/25-ways-to-fight-your-storys-mushy-middle/

Ending With a Bang

The ending of a book is important because it influences everything that went before—and because in industry parlance: "The first pages sell the book. The last pages sell the next book." A happy ending is not a necessity for an artistic book, although it may be required in some genres, such as romance or romantic suspense, but the ending must be satisfying or the reader will feel cheated.

What is a satisfying ending? An ending that has been earned, by the protagonist's efforts and not artificially created by the author's godlike hand. An ending for which the reader has been prepared with hints and seeds dropped throughout the book that the reader may not consciously have noticed but absorbed nonetheless. An ending that, even if a surprise, makes sense to the reader within the confines of the book's world and is not a blast of insanity from out of nowhere simply for shock value.

A pantser—even a partial outliner like me—won't know the ending until s/he reaches it, so these next practices may end up being useful only at the end of the first draft. Still, I would encourage you to think seriously—on paper—about your book's ending at whatever stage you find yourself.

Final Exercises

1. Write the last few scenes early on, rather than waiting until the end. You'll change the scenes later, but at least you've got some material to work with and a destination to journey towards.

2. Write two or three alternative possible endings.

3. Write an ending from another character's point of

view (even that of a non-point-of-view character).

4. Write an ending as though you are setting up a sequel.

5. Try an unintended consequence, like killing off a character you hadn't intended to kill, or letting one survive you had planned on killing off. Even if you don't use this, it might give inspiration to change something else.

Must-Read Books for Writers

I have a larger collection of books on creative writing than most college libraries own. I have been collecting, reading, and studying them all my life. And in one way or another, I have found them all useful.

Some recapitulate concepts, techniques, and tips from many other books, but they will perhaps have one I haven't yet encountered—or they will express one or more I've met before in such a way that it sinks in more deeply than it did when I ran across it earlier. So I count those books still successful for me, if in small ways. Many of the books I own deal with specific kinds of writing or with specific techniques—mysteries and suspense, science fiction, dialogue, plotting—and I've often found them extremely useful, frequently return to the best of them again and again.

When I wanted to narrow down my books to a most-critical shortlist for this book, I found that repeatedly the books that shot to the top were books that dealt with the writing process as a whole, with being a writer and living a writer's life. Each will have some specific techniques within, but the book as a whole is about the process of becoming and being a writer. They deal with overcoming negativity and fear, dealing with belittling from others, developing the discipline necessary to make a life as a writer, defeating the intimidation of starting a big project, and in one blessed case, how to make a writing life within the business of writing and publishing.

These are the books I recommend again and again to students and friends, to anyone who asks me for advice and help. They are books I still go back to time and again. They're not the only good books on writing. I never get rid of any of my vast collection of writing books because they all have at least one thing to offer me. But these books are the ones I would keep if I could suddenly only have twelve books on writing in my library.

Carolyn See's *Making a Literary Life* is at the top of the list because it is such a little gem. I've bought so many copies of this book to give to aspiring writers. I only wish it had been available to me earlier in my career. By the time, I discovered it I'd learned some of what it teaches the hard way. It rings true in all of its suggestions and guidelines because See is a successful writer and teacher who's writing from experience. *Making a Literary Life* deals with things few other books do, such as how to have a writing career when you live far from the epicenter of publishing in New York or how to develop friendships and connections with literary and publishing colleagues if you know no one. This last may seem easier to do now that social media is available, but See's suggestions in this area are even more relevant in a time when a handwritten note is remarkable. If I can recommend or give only one book, this is the one I choose.

Dorothea Brande's *Becoming a Writer* is the other book I'd give if only allowed to give two. Published in the 1930s and long out of print, award-winning novelist John Gardner swore by it and mentioned its importance in one of his own books on writing (see below), which led to it being reissued with a foreword by Gardner. This book deals with the psychology of the writer, with how to develop the confidence, the focus, and the discipline any writer needs and how to learn what your own material, your individual forte as a writer, is. It teaches us techniques to connect with our creativity and learn to see and experience the world as writers. It would be worth a fortune for its technique of "Act As If" alone, which has been picked up by many other writing gurus and self-help authors.

It also offers the initial appearance of the fruitful technique of freewriting first thing in the morning (later built on by Natalie Goldberg and Julia Cameron among others). This book is a lifesaver for writers.

These two, above all the others, are immensely helpful to anyone who wants to write as more than a hobby. For the rest of the books on the list, I have no definite order. They offer different things to the writer and fill different needs, so it wasn't workable for me to rank them by importance. Each would leave an important hole in my writing library if it were missing, however.

Uber-best-selling Stephen King's *On Writing: A Memoir of the Craft* is one of the best general guides to writing extant. A master class in a book, it's a tiny treasure house of useful and pithy advice on everything from getting and taking feedback, individual techniques like description, plot, and character, how to organize a workspace and structure your day's work to his stricture on reading that I love to quote to students: "If you don't have time to read, you don't have the time (or the tools) to write. Simple as that." And this is definitely one of the books you need to make time to read.

Natalie Goldberg's *Writing Down the Bones* marries Dorothea Brande's freewriting morning pages technique to her own intensive yoga background to build a tremendously useful set of practices for writers to follow. This book focuses on getting in touch with your own creative spirit and defeating resistance and fear. It's more modern in outlook than Brande's and the borrowings from yoga are quite useful. It takes the important foundations of Brande's book and adds to them, but you won't find all those foundations here, so though I recommend this book highly, if you have to make a choice of only one, get Brande's. (Julia Cameron has taken the same techniques and added another layer of

12-step spirituality and dogma to them in *The Artist's Way*. Many have found that helpful to them, as well, but again you won't find all the important fundamentals Brande gives you in *The Artist's Way*, either.)

Award-winning children's book author Madeleine L'Engle's *A Circle of Quiet* is an intimate little book, the first of her Crosswicks Journals series. A meditative book about life and writing, it's also a book about failure and rejection, about feeling guilty for taking time to write when earning no money from it, about the collision of family and writing, and about the humility that good writing requires. Some of the most important things I've taken from this book have been her focus on using journals and writer's notebooks to do various writing exercises, which she gives you in the book, and her stress that real artists keep studying, practicing, and learning all the time in order to keep growing. You can learn much from this book, and it's the ultimate writer's comfort book when feeling down.

Leonard Bishop's *Dare to Be a Great Writer* is a big book with a big title. Bishop was a grade-school dropout, thief, and hobo who became a critically acclaimed novelist and friend of Norman Mailer and Joseph Heller before becoming one of the top-rated writing professors in the country. His big, brash book is blunt in its advice, which ranges from discipline and structuring your life around writing to tons of techniques from tiny to large, from smooth sentence transitions to genre structures. This is a fabulous writer's reference. Each separate entry is in alphabetical order and thus easy to look up and refer to. My copy sits next to my desk marked with a rainbow of Post-Its and bookmarks.

Bestselling mystery novelist Elizabeth George's *Write Away: One Writer's Approach to Fiction and the Writing Life* is aimed at the writer of mysteries and crime fiction, but offers great help for all novelists. George provides another master class in this book with a detailed overview of how to construct a novel, a step-by-step analysis of her process from idea to final edits, and help with all kinds of technique, using examples from her own work and that of other commercial and literary novelists. Again, this is a book I return to time and again, always learning something. An example of one of her unique technique helps is THADs, Talking Head Avoidance Devices, ways to occupy characters when they must have a critical dialogue so that more happens on the page than just the dreaded talking heads as in a public affairs TV show.

Brenda Ueland's *If You Want to Write: A Book about Art, Independence, and Spirit* is another older book, one that Carl Sandburg called "the best book ever written about how to write." This is a book about tapping into your own creative spirit and delight. Her chapter titles alone are a treatise on the writing life. Here are two examples: "Everybody is Talented, Original and Has Something Important to Say" and "Why Women Who Do Too Much Housework Should Neglect It for Their Writing." She stresses that any creative gift increases as we use it and with some lazy time, which she calls "moodling" and insists is critical to the really important big, slow ideas. Read this book to help find your creative center.

John Gardner's *On Becoming a Novelist* is hugely helpful to novelists in particular. Gardner is widely considered one of the great American novelists of the 20th century, and he taught many other critically acclaimed writers, such as Raymond Carver. Gardner, as I mentioned earlier, was responsible for bringing Dorothea Brande's book back from obscurity, and his own book is a grand follow-up to hers, but aimed at novelists and not all writers. Gardner goes deeply into the need to create a kind of dream-state in the reader's mind as well as the benefits of repeated revisions. There's much in here about making a writer's life for yourself today and much as well about the benefits and difficulties for novelists of MFA program that are centered on poetry and short fiction.

Annie Dillard's *The Writing Life* is, like, Stephen King's book, part autobiography of the writer and part guidebook to the world of the working writer. Though not as absolutely useful in practical terms to the writer as King's book, Dillard's is full of strange beauties and a real sense of the writer as one who is, or should be, dedicated spiritually to her art. One of my favorite writing quotes comes from this book: "Spend it all, shoot it, play it, lose it, all, right away, every time. Do not hoard what seems good for a later place in the book, or for another book; give it, give it all, give it now."

These are the ten gems of my collection that I originally recommended to all of my classes. I've since added two other books to the list. The first is a new book just recently published, *Writes of Passage*, a collection of essays from successful writers (including me) who are members of the national writers organization, Sisters in Crime, essays about almost every aspect of writing a novel in general and mysteries in particular. These essays cover craft issues, problem-solving tips, the business of writing, as well as inspiration and encouragement for the inevitable slough of despond.

The second is a book by the great master storyteller, Ursula K. Le Guin, called *Steering the Craft: Exercises and Discussions on Story Writing for the Lone Navigator or the Mutinous Crew*. Le Guin takes issue with the prominence of conflict as a necessity in modern novels and pushes for change as the catalyst of story instead. She explains each aspect of craft in lucid terms, illustrating it with excerpts from great writers, such as Virginia Woolf, J.R.R. Tolkien, and Mark Twain, and offers charming and challenging exercises. This book is a self-directed master class with one of the finest writers living.

You may, like me, be a collector of books about writing, but even if you never buy or check out from the library any books on writing other than these, you will want these twelve books, and you will find them helpful over and over again.

Sample Documents

These documents are all actual samples of ones I have used in writing my own published novels. I have left them as they are, so if you are familiar with, for example, *Every Last Secret*, you will find in some early ones that it is called *Every Secret Thing*, and you will find that early outlines or plot documents discuss whole chapters that never made it into the final book. If you are familiar with *Every Broken Trust*, you will find in early documents a totally different set of murderers and another plot planned than the one used in the final book.

I have included these documents because my students have always found them helpful for two reasons. The first is that they can see the technique or element of craft we have been discussing in actual use. The second is that they can see samples of some of the mess and chaos that occurs backstage in the writing of a novel. I have left in the mistakes and errors, as well, for that very purpose.

Too often, we see only the finished product of the novel in the bookstore or library and despair when we look from its professional, pristine state to our own messy, confused notes and drafts. It is human nature, and yet the bane of every writer, to compare his fragmentary, heavily corrected, and constantly changed work in progress to the professionally edited, copy-edited, and proofread book in its professionally designed and printed pages. This is rather like comparing a cake in the midst of mixing ingredients together in the bowl to a professionally baked and decorated cake.

It helps, I've always found, to see that professional

novelists make just as much mess and just as many mistakes along the way to the finished product as you are doing now. I hope these sample documents will make it seem more possible for you to write your own successful novel.

~~What happened to Jake?~~

~~Why is Brian with Skeet?~~

~~What happened to Julie, Brian, and Skeet last year?~~

Will Joe and Skeet get together?

~~Why had Brian had to be a grownup too soon?~~

Why does Walker need a mercenary like Terry?

Will Joe and Terry come to blows?

Does Skeet accept her Cherokee heritage?

What's going on between Walker and Liz?

~~Who's Randy after?~~

~~What happened to Karen?~~

What does Skeet know that turned her against Jeremy?

~~What were Karen and Leonard doing in the Caves?~~

Was Leonard followed to Brewster to be killed?

Was Leonard's death connected to the scene with Leonard at the party?

~~What had Leonard known that made murder worthwhile?~~

~~Why did Karen lie to Skeet and sneak off to the Caves?~~

Was Leonard corrupt due to his drinking?

Who killed Jake and why?

Where did Ignacio get the Banana Slugs T-shirt?

Where did Karen find Ignacio?

Who is Ignacio really?

Did Walker kill Miryam's old rich man?

Why does Walker need Terry?

Is Jeremy in love with Skeet?

Who left the party early?

Where did the gun come from?

What did Leonard know?
Why not kill Karen, too?
Whose car did the killer see?
Will Joe win Skeet?
Will Sam win Skeet back?

Sample of First Draft Notes Document

This document ran to 44 pages
EVERY LAST SECRET
Notes
CHECK THIS EVERY DAY AND DURING REWRITES

Make sure there is a cause for every single event or action in book, and that there is then a corresponding effect, which will be the cause of something else.

Stimulus must external—action, dialogue, something seen. Response must be external. For every stimulus, you must show a response, and for every desired response, you must provide a stimulus.

The response usually must follow the stimulus at once.

When the response to stimulus is not logical on the surface, you must ordinarily explain it.

STIMULUS--INTERNALIZATION--RESPONSE

Internalization is caused by a stimulus. It doesn't "just happen." Internalization belongs between stimulus and response.

Sensory descriptions should be sprinkled throughout, not put in a lump. First, sight, second, hearing, third, smell. Use for sight, spatial dimension, source of light, color, visual texture. Use for hearing, loudness, tone, complexity, direction and distance. Use for smell, soothing, stinging, choking, evocative adjectives—find good descriptors.

Use omniscient descriptions when no character can see or experience the whole scene, or it will be much simpler and more vivid outside the limited viewpoint. Then, use only at the beginning of chapters or scenes when there's been a break in action or time and no viewpoint has yet been established.

Afterward, all further description must be from inside the character viewpoint.

3/10/04

What is the problem I'm having with the book right now?

Plot and structure—these are always my difficulties. I can write smooth, easy-reading prose for hours at a time. I cannot quite as automatically create lifelike characters and give them realistic dialogue.

It's action that is my problem. I can do scenes that make the reader feel as if he or she is there, but too often there's nothing really interesting or exciting happening in these scenes.

Structure and pacing—these are my problems. It's not really just a matter of plot. I can come up with a logical storyline of events to happen, but it always seems as if they're either packed too close together—bam! bam! bam!—or the story meanders through meals and meetings and conversations and thoughts and memories without any real action taking place.

Look at *Dead Man* so far. The first chapter has plenty of action with the brief scenes of Andrew's blackmailing and other blackguardery. Then the first scene of chapter two has a bang-up argument between Skeet and her ex that also brings out a lot of information about her past. After that, there's a scene of nothing but talk with no conflict or real furthering of plot. Then a fight with Andrew and Scott is a small part of an otherwise boring lunch scene.

After that comes a scene with police staff that should be interesting with an argument between Skeet and Frank, but I can't seem to write it. And, anyway, it won't really further the plot. Then the supper scene with Joe and Julie, which I need, but which has no action but just conversation again. Then Skeet at home with Mike coming by to talk about the VC covering up Andrew's embezzlement.

Finally, after all this TALK, TALK, TALK, comes the scene where the body's discovered—and it takes place in a telephone call!

Can I see a problem with all this? Oh, yeah. The even bigger problem, however, is what to do about it.

Possibility A = Throw in some action, even if it seems arbitrary to me right now. The old bring-in-a-man-with-a-gun trick.

Possibility B = Get rid of everything except the scenes that have some conflict and further plot immediately, which would be Skeet's fight with her ex, the fight between Andrew and Scott, and the call about the body.

Possibility C = Show body being found. (This doesn't speak to the slow pace before this scene, of course.)

Possibility D = Put some conflict or action and some plot relevance in each of the scenes up to this point.

Possibility E = Add more subplot action/conflict in these early scenes, thus enriching the book and keeping it from being boring while setting up the murder.

Possibility F = Rethink the whole plot. Make it more of a suspense novel or thriller than a mystery per se, with scenes of the villain engaged in evil deeds from the beginning.

Possibility G = A combination of two or more of these possibilities, such as A, D, E, F, and maybe C.

If I rethink the entire plot and make it more of a thriller, I'll focus more on Stuart from the beginning and show him doing dastardly things with/to kids from the beginning. Cutting brief scenes of those in with the early scenes should help keep interest high. In fact, it pretty much takes care of Possibility A, as well.

If, then, I add more subplot action/conflict to the early scenes, thus also fulfilling Possibility D, the whole beginning ought to move faster.

Do I really want to make this a thriller, as opposed to a mystery, though?

What if I keep showing scenes of all the suspects doing suspicious or dastardly things? Could that give me some of the suspense of the thriller and keep the mystery?

I guess I'm suspicious of the impulse to turn it into a thriller because I suspect a great deal of that derives from laziness or lack of confidence. Not wanting to deal with the more demanding plot/structure requirements of the mystery. And I know fulfilling them would be good for me since plotting/structure/pacing are always my weakest points.

Or what if I show Stuart without saying who's doing these things—from deep inside his consciousness? Would that be playing unfair with the reader? Think of *Night Sins* and others like it, Julie Garwood's latest, etc. Can I do that?

Sample of First Draft Journal Document

This document ran 74 pages. Ones like it were kept for each draft of the book.

Journal of Every Broken Trust First Draft

February 22, 2010

I'm starting to play around with the 2nd in my Brewster, MO, series featuring Skeet Bannion. I know Molly Wise's husband was actually murdered, and Molly will find out somehow—**HOW???**—at the beginning of this book. Jake Wise found out about a dangerous conspiracy—**WHAT???**—with some players—**WHO???**—even in his own agency—**WHAT???**. He was killed—**HOW???**—but it was made to look like an accident—**HOW??** ALL ANSWERED

I have to answer these questions before I have a story. This is all backstory, but these same people will be trying to kill Molly and then Skeet. Because this is all still going on, and when Molly starts trying to find out who was responsible for Jake's death and gets threatened, maybe beat up, Skeet will have to find out what's going on to protect Molly and avenge father-figure Jake.

So all of this is important. I'm thinking Jake was an assistant U.S. Attorney for Missouri's Western District. They're dealing with human trafficking, drug dealing, interstate gangs.

I think I'll use *Above the Law* as a working title.

February 23, 2010

Skeet is mostly recovered from surgery on her leg after

being shot by Stuart Morley. She has been able to gain custody of Brian, which will be made into an adoption in a year. Jeremy got Brian out of a ghastly foster home and took into his own home as foster parents until Skeet could regain Brian legally. Therefore, Brian and Skeet both owe Jeremy a debt of gratitude, which doesn't sit well with Skeet, who knows Jeremy'a a real twister. Skeet's also checking on her dad a couple of times a week. He's back in his house now with a physical therapist coming most days and Sam checking on him the days Skeet doesn't.

How can I keep this mystery tied to Brewster and the campus? **Done** Have Molly attacked after being told by Leonard in underground part of campus? At beginning **done** Have someone key to the murder of Jake and the conspiracy in Brewster, even on Chouteau campus—New dean of Law School, former U.S. Attorney, previously Jake's boss and friend—George "Mel" Melvin. He's just been named Dean of the Law School, after a failed political race. Molly considers him a friend and a friend of Jake's. Skeet knows him—Does she like him? No Why not?

Is he the ultimate murderer or a vctim? Involved with murder of Jake but eventually a victim. Why is he killed? **Done.** Have Mel killed on the campus—How? When? Why? Have suspects in the Brewster/Chouteau community as well as in Kansas City.

Three murders to solve—Jake's in the past, Leonard Klamath's in the underground part of the campus because he told Molly the truth—at beginning, Mel's on campus— early on. First two connected with the conspiracy—What??? Human trafficking? Mel's murder by someone in Brewster for personal reasons/greed/etc.

Molly can be a suspect in Mel's murderMolly also attacked on her farm—Ignacio calls Skeet and tries to free her. Does

Molly involve Brian somehow with her quest, endangering him and causing friction between Skeet and Molly and Skeet and Brian?

When does this all take place? Spring in *Every Secret Thing*, so now it's late summer/early fall, new semester starting.

Molly gives a party for her friend the new Dean and invites old buddies from KC as well as Webster friends. She gives it at Skeet's house so folks won't have to tramp out to her farm. This is where now-alcoholic Leonard Klamath gets drunk and insists Molly meet him in the underground to tell her the truth about Jake's death.

Molly intends to find Jake's murderer and bring him to justice. Skeet intends to protect Molly and find Jake's/ Leonard's murderer and bring him to justice and to find Mel's murderer.

Was Mel the actual murderer of Jake at Walker Lynch's behest? This will make Molly look more guilty.

Who is Walker Lynch? More powerful than Mel was as US Attorney. Ultra-rich. Community benefactor. No one knows where his money comes from. Where does Walker's original money come from??? He funds several charities that work with immigrants, domestic violence, and the homeless, especially runaway teens. Perfect fronts for trafficking.

Who does Walker have kill Leonard and beat up Molly? Terry Heldrich, his driver/bodyguard.

What's the motive for killing Mel? Who does it? He's abusive and jealous of his much younger and richer wife Liz Richar. She made him sign a prenup agreement, but she's having an affair, and if he proves it, he can divorce her and get a big sum of money from her. She married him because she thought he'd be a political winner. Now, she wants free to marry a rising political star, Randy Thorsson, newly appointed state senator, with whom she's been having an affair. Walker is her longtime lover and has agreed to bankroll Randy's career when they are married.

Pay attention in the book to place. We have the fancy expensive suburb where Randy and Mel live that backs up on the north of the wildlife preserve—3 scenes. We have the wildlife preserve. We have the town square with Molly's shop and Pyewacket's Café and Mother Earth Books and The Herbal Coffeeshop—3 scenes. We have the Missouri River and the Riverwalk—3 scenes. We have the Kansa Reservation across the river. We have the campus—3 scenes. We have Molly's sheep and goat farm—3 scenes.

What grows here and what doesn't?

Sample Character Freewriting

(This is a sample of a document that ran 6 pages.)
REV MATT TALKS

My bottom line is always Jean. She's everything to me. I would do anything for her. I don't understand why it is that the more I do for her, the less she loves me. I was drowning in blood-guilt when I met her. It was her passion for others and her glowing, innate goodness that drew me to her like a drowning man to a lifebuoy. I wasn't sure if God would save me after all I'd done, but I knew Jean would. She became the center, the plumb line of my life. As long as I had her goodness, I was saved from the evil I had done, the evil I had become. So you can understand why I couldn't afford to lose her.

I didn't mean to kill Jake—though the bastard had it coming. Unfaithful to his own wife and making my wife cheat on me with him. I just wanted to tell him to stay away from my wife. All right, maybe I wanted to slug him a time or two. He deserved it, damn it! The thought of him touching my Jean, undressing her, fucking her. Hell, it all makes me want to kill him all over again. But I didn't mean to kill him that night. I just wanted to scare him away from her and get a little of my own back.

I waited until he'd taken me upstairs. He was trying to keep things quiet, and I'd threatened to make a loud scene or tell his wife if he didn't talk to me. As soon as we left the stairs, I started hitting him. Didn't say anything. I didn't want anyone to hear. The first two blows knocked him off his feet. I swear I'd have stopped with the next one if it hadn't lifted him up and knocked him down the stairs. He fell down both flights. Over and over. I couldn't believe it. I just stood there, staring in dumb silence. When he didn't get up, I ran down to him. He didn't seem to be breathing, and his face was turning blue, but he had a real weak heartbeat. I realized he would probably die or certainly be permanently disabled. I've seen guys in that state before. They'd arrest me. I panicked and broke his neck without thinking about it. Just did it. Like you did for buddies who were too hurt to make it back to base with you.

I went out that back door he'd let me in, shaking like a new recruit after his first battle. Next day, Leonard Klamath got hold of me. Said he'd been there when I called Jake, that he knew I'd had a hand in Jake's death, and he started blackmailing me. It seemed just. I had sinned so horribly. I'd have to pay this bloodsucker all my life. Fair punishment.

Then Jean tried to kill herself. I knew I had to make things change, come right. So I quit my job and took the pastorage of the little Brewster church. I worked like a dog to get it, to move us, to set up a shop for Jean, anything to make things better for her, to make it all come right with her and me again.

But it wasn't. And I started to think that she had never really loved me, not like she loved him. That was scary. It made me so angry with her. I didn't want to go there. So I just tried harder. Then Leonard Klamath showed up at that party and started mouthing off. Old drunk!

I couldn't let him tell Karen or anyone. I'd paid him plenty for his silence, damn it! I slipped out the kitchen door when you took him out front. I got Jean's gun from her glove compartment. I was ready to follow his car, but he went up the hill on foot so I followed him. I shot him in the caves. He was obviously waiting for someone. I couldn't let that meeting take place. Then suddenly, Karen was there. I hid behind a car. I didn't want to shoot her, too. She was a sufferer from Jake's sin with my wife, just as I was. Besides, I'd already killed her husband. I couldn't shoot her. She found Leonard and started to make a call. I knocked her out and ran away.

Sample of Freewriting Plot Document

This document ran to 26 pages over several different sessions of working out problems at various stages of the plot.

FREEWRITING ON *Every Broken Trust* PLOT

Where do I want to go from this beginning of the book? I'm at the end of Chapter 6. That makes for a long beginning. Actually, only Chapter 1 was set-up. Chapter 2 had the murder. Chapter 3 on has been early investigation and trying to care for & protect Karen.

Not enough action and conflict going on in those chapters, though. Obstacles or conflicts must grow worse each time Skeet deals with the last one successfully (or not).

Conflict in Chapter 1 **between Skeet & Karen over party**. Conflict in Chapter 1 **between Joe & Terry**.

Conflict in Chapter 2 between **Skeet & Karen**. Conflict in Chapter 2 **between Skeet & Jeremy, Leonard & Karen, Leonard & Mel, Leonard & Skeet.**

Conflict in Chapter 3 between Skeet & Dud, Gil & Dud. Conflict in Chapter 3 between **Skeet & Angie**, Skeet & Karen.

Conflict in Chapter 4 between **Skeet & Karen**. Conflict in Chapter 4 between Skeet & Annette & Miryam.

Conflict in Chapter 5 **between Skeet & Jeremy & Chancellor**. Conflict in Chapter 5 **between Skeet & Karen.**

Conflict in Chapter 6 **between Angie & Mel & Liz**. Conflict **between Liz & Mel.**

Not enough, but with the exception of adding Walker &

Terry to Chapter 6, it can all wait until the first revision.

Where am I going to go now? I have to speed things up. I have to have **much more and stronger** conflict happening. I need to have everything pointing toward Mel, so his murder in Chapter 9 not only incriminates Karen but throws Skeet back past her starting point.

DO I REALLY NEED DENISE ACTING IN THE BOOK? no

The primary purpose of the plot is to give the protagonist a reason to change in the direction she needs to change.

Skeet has to learn to have patience and understanding with the shortcomings and failings of others. This means she will have to be forced to forgive and understand Karen and Brian.

An outline of the events that demonstrate the protagonist's external and internal problems, show the rising conflict and increasing stakes, and come to crisis, climax, and resolution. Think EVENT~ actual discrete happenings where the protagonist interacts, makes decisions, confronts an obstacle, investigates, enlists an ally, makes an enemy, gives into temptation, searches for something missing, breaks the rules... some action that manifests the protagonist's personality and purpose. Don't forget that each event will have consequences that will bring on the next event.

Who is the real murderer? Terry. Who is the real mastermind? Walker. Who else is involved? Mel and Liz.

What really happened with Jake's murder?

The Story of the Murders and the Murderers

Sample of Scene Analysis Document

1st page only—runs for several pages

EVERY SECRET THING
Scene Analysis

Chapter 1
1.   In the middle of the night, Skeet gets call about body and leaves house.
2.   Scene of crime—Gil. M.E., evidence techs—hole in wall, trophy, footprint, unlocked French window.

Chapter 2
1.   Skeet tells Tina and Brian—finds out Andrew did research for Oldrick.
2.   Skeet knits and thinks about murder and unanswered questions.

Chapter 3
1.   At coffee shop next morning, Skeet makes list of questions and suspects.
2.   Mike Berman tells her Andrew's prosecution has been cancelled by Eugene—Skeet asks him to recreate documents he gave to Eugene's office.
3   Sam and Skeet fight over her move, her job, and Charlie.
4.   Skeet analyzes argument and realizes that something is wrong with Charlie, calls Charlie to schedule meeting.
5.   Stuart asks Skeet for date again after complaining about seeing her with Joe and Julie
6.   Miryam tell her Andrew asked about KC photographers.

Chapter 4

1. Skeet and chancellor fight about covering up murder—Jeremy tries to get her to report everything, she refuses.

2. Skeet tells Frank to handle media.

3. Skeet questions Janice and learns about porn angle of research for Oldick.

Chapter 5

1. At bookstore, Miryam tells Skeet about porn photographers and about Andrew's amethyst.

2. Skeet questions Oldrick—learns Andrew found porn connection and Stuart stopped research.

Chapter 6

1. Skeet questions Scott—learns about the accounts article that Andrew took—Skeet asks Scott to recreate research.

2. Skeet questions Duran—he's hiding something.

Chapter 7

2. Jeremy tries to get information out of Skeet.

3. Skeet finds Charlie sick—he wants to help with the murder—they fight.

Chapter 8

1. At Tom's house, Skeet and Gil question him and take him in when they find possible murder weapon.

2. Tina tells Skeet of strange papers of Andrew's.

Sample of Chapter Outline Document

This document ran to 8 pages

Every Broken Trust **Chapter Outline**

ACT ONE
26ppChapter One14
THURSDAY   10Scene 1 - EVENT **Skeet & Karen** argue over party—they go to The Herbal for lunch w/ **Annette and Miryam** and **Leonard** comes in to talk to Karen but won't when he sees Skeet—+

17Scene 2 - Skeet picks up **Brian** after work and heads to Pyewacket's for supper where they join **Joe and Julie**— **Mel, Liz, Walker, Terry** come in—Walker & Terry come over—Walker introduces Terry, who shows interest in Skeet— EVENT Joe and Terry wind up bristling at each other— Bob & Kathy Lynch try to meet and talk to Walker on his way out of Pyewacket's & Terry foils them ++

27ppChapter Two14
SUNDAY   10Scene 1 - EVENT Skeet, Brian, Karen getting ready for party—in come guests **Bob & Kathy Lynch**, Mel and Liz, **Jeremy**, Miryam, Annette, **Helen & Rev. Matt Lawson**, Walker and Terry, **Randy**—Bob & Kathy ask Walker about his heritage, trying to establish connection and Walker is uncomfortable and wary—+

15Scene 2 - Skeet w/ Helen, then Annette, then Joe—she sees Leonard making drunk nuisance of self—Karen & Helen go to soothe him—EVENT he yells about **Jake**—Helen gets shook up & runs to hide—Mel tries to shut him up—Skeet makes Leonard leave but before he does he whispers to Karen that Jake was murdered and he'd meet her in the Caves to tell her who—Karen goes to kitchen to call cab—+++--Skeet and Jeremy spar—she and Joe talk when suddenly her cell rings and it's Karen, scared and abruptly cut off—Skeet and Joe head to the Caves—++++

2Scene 3— EVENT Skeet and Joe find Karen unconscious in the Caves next to Leonard's body—Skeet calls for ambulance and night sergeant—Karen taken to hospital in ambulance—+++++

20ppChapter Three14

9Scene 1 – At hospital, EVENT Skeet finds Brian with **Angie**, whose mother overdosed outside Mel's house later after the murder—**FROM ANGIE'S FIRST SCENES, SHE MUST BE SEEN SNOOPING, CONSTANTLY TEXTING, PHOTOGRAPHING, AND RECORDING WITH HER IPHONE.** —Brian tells Skeet about phone message from Coreen—Skeet finally gets to take Karen home— ++++++

10Scene 2 - Skeet takes Karen home and EVENT charges **Ignacio** to watch over her—Karen insists that Jake was murdered and Skeet has to find out who did it—Skeet says she has to find out who killed Leonard, and if Jake was killed, it will be the same person—Karen is sure Mel knows what happened—she urges Skeet to talk to Dan in KC to get them to reopen Jake's case—Skeet says okay, she's got to go check on Charlie anyway—+++++++

Sample of Writing Notebook

[I originally kept this as a huge 3-ring binder—and still use that when looking something up for the next book in the series. I tried to convert it to a computer doc and found it didn't work well for me, so I went to separate documents. But you might find this more useful. And when setting up a new world for a series, I still set up a big binder with these and more categories and fill in by hand at first.]

Title Ideas
Death of a Student Journalist
Dying for News
A Quiet Little Murder
DEAD MAN ON CAMPUS
Every Secret Thing

Last verse of Ecclesiastes: "for God shall bring every work into judgment, with every secret thing, whether it be good, or whether it be evil."
(new page)

Chronology

Skeet graduates from high school in Oklahoma and comes to KC to go to police academy.

Skeet marries Sam in

Skeet divorces Sam in

Skeet graduates with B.S. in

Skeet makes homicide detective in

Skeet graduates with M.A. in

Skeet becomes Metro Division Watch Commander in

Skeet's dad forced into retirement by Internal Affairs in

Skeet takes job in Webster with Chouteau University in

(new page)

Situation

Skeet becomes Chief of Campus Police for Chouteau College (now University) 6 months before story begins. Frank Booth, her second-in-command, is older and sullen. He resents her being chosen over him, although his only experience is as a campus policeman and traditionally chiefs of campus forces are chosen from experienced regular police officers. Joe Louzon became the Chief of Police for Webster a year before after working his way up the ranks. Joe has been friendly and accepting of Skeet, showing admiration and some romantic interest. Mike Berman, Assistant Professor of English, also is a friend and potential suitor. Skeet is running from a very successful career in homicide and administration with the Kansas City Missouri Police Department after Internal Affairs determined that her father, a lifer on the force, was corrupt and forced him to retire.

Andrew McAfee is the editor of the campus newspaper, *The Chouteau News*. Andrew has had two big public fights already this week – one with a woman student writing for the paper whom he sexually harassed and one with the male news editor, Scott Lampkin, who had his research for an investigative article disappear from his desk and the files after he mentioned what he was working on to Andrew.

Andrew also had a more private fight with Dean Tom Jamison, his wife's ex-husband. Tom has discovered that Andrew is cheating on Tina and stealing her blind and called him on it. Tina doesn't know, however.

Andrew is studying with Alec Oldick (Mirkin/Dilks type) and involved with his "research" in pedophilia/child pornography. Andrew's also blackmailing Stuart Morley (T. Burns-type) for his child porn involvement.

Finally, Assistant Professor Mike Berman, the faculty

advisor for *The Chouteau News,* discovers that Andrew's embezzling from the paper's operating funds. When Mike goes to Alice Fremantle, the Assistant to the Vice Chancellor for Student Development, she's gung-ho to take it to Gene Scheuer, the VC, and nail Andrew. A day later, she tells Mike to forget it and covers it up. All because Andrew has used the research of Scott to uncover a longstanding web of embezzlement by the three vice chancellors and the Dean of Humanities (the old chancellor was in on it and the current head of accounting is also). Andrew arranges a meeting with the VCs and Dean to blackmail them and, incidentally, have his own charges dismissed.

Andrew is found dead in his editor's office early Tuesday morning by one of Skeet's night shift. He was killed with a blow to the head that crushed his skull late Monday night. (new page)

Theme

Secrets are often destructive and can be deadly.

Users and manipulators eventually are punished.

The guilty must be caught to protect the innocent from direct harm and from suspicion.

(new page)

Background

See maps of town square and college.

Brewster, Missouri, is

River Walk Park

Missouri River

Kansa Reservation

Old Brewster

Kensington

Wickbrook—expensive suburb where many faculty live

BREWSTER TOWN SQUARE

√ Forgotten Arts—fiber/quilting store with classrooms–

Molly Wise, owner, Cherry Ebersol, student and part-time clerk

√The Herbal Coffee Shop—coffee shop with bakery and cooking/ornamental herb shop—Dolores Ramirez, owner, Ellie Jenkins, cook, Kurt Wagener and Margo Ramey, students and part-time help

√Mother Earth Bookstore—feminist/New Age bookstore—Carolyn Ehrlich and Miryam Rainbow, owners, Carla Hubert and Tanya Flach, students and part-time help

√Pyewacket Café—organic, counterculture restaurant gone upscale—Pal and Sandi Owens, owners, aging hippies in long graying ponytails and Birkenstocks all year round—multiple student waiters and cooks

Tintagel Gallery-upscale art gallery—Danielle (Dani) Sathoff, owner

Forster's Antiques—exclusive antiques store—Charles and Helen Forster, owners

√Art's—long-established bar and grill with working-class clientele—townie establishment that Dani and Bea and Forsters have been trying to force off the square—Art Williamson owns and bartends, Ray Campbell cooks, Twyla Koenig, longtime waitress

√Aunt Bea's Antiques and Collectibles—owned by Bea Roberts, sweet-faced bitch

√The World In Your Hands—international goods—owned by Sally Lawson, ex-S.L., wife of Reverend Matt Lawson of Methodist Church

(Many more pages—new page)

CAMPUS POLICE SQUAD ROOM

Public is buzzed in through locked door after asking at [protected] window. The squad room is long and wide with several desks off to one side that are shared by patrol officers for filling out paperwork, etc. Immediately across from the entrance door is an office for Lt. Gil Mendez, next to that an office shared by the three sergeants for the three shifts, then an office for Captain Frank Booth. Turn the corner and you have a wall with windows against which are the desk for the dispatcher and the desk for the secretary. Turn the corner again and you have Skeet's office, then a conference room. Further on, against the walls are monitors for the security cameras on campus.

Three shifts = 7-3 with 1 sergeant, 1 dispatcher, 6 patrol officers, 3-11 with 1 sergeant, 1 dispatcher, 6 patrol officers, 11-7 with 1 sergeant, 1 dispatcher, 2 patrol officers, plus 8-5 with chief, captain, lieutenant, and secretary.

15,000 students at Chouteau University and 3,000 faculty and staff.

ANDREW MACAFEE'S OFFICE

Andrew sits at a small battered desk with old wooden captain's chair on wheels and two visitor's chairs in front. On the desk are a computer monitor and keyboard with CPU tower on floor. A printer and scanner and fax machine sit on the horizontal file cabinet behind the desk. Tall, old vertical file cabinets stand on each side of that horizontal file.

The door to the *Chouteau News* newsroom is opposite the desk. A tall bookcase stands next to the long, low French windows on the wall to the left-hand side of the desk. A waist-high bookcase topped with a work counter runs the length of the wall to the right of the desk.

Items on counter=

Items on desk= Amethyst geode, Maori carving from New Zealand, papers and files, phone, computer and monitor

Diagram of room

(new page)

Characters

Marquitta (Skeet) Bannion

Skeet is tall (5'8") and athletic with a lean, muscular body and broad shoulders. Underneath her short, dark hair, her Cherokee heritage shows in her strong features, huge, dark eyes and heavy eyebrows. Her mother was half Cherokee and returned to Oklahoma with Skeet after the divorce to live near Tahlequah. Skeet's father, Charlie Bannion, was a cop from a family of cops in Kansas City. Skeet visited her father and his family on holidays and every summer. She played basketball in high school, going to state championships. After graduation, she came to Kansas City to become a police officer like her father, much to his dismay since he didn't think women belonged in police work. She moved up through the ranks while earning a college degree and marrying, then divorcing a fellow officer. She was a homicide detective for years while earning a master's degree. Eventually, she moved into administration and became Watch Commander for the Central Patrol Division.

Skeet has had to learn the hard way to control her temper, which she inherited from her father who never learned to control his. She hates what some cops do but loves what police can mean to a society and to individuals. Everyone thought she was on her way up the administrative ladder to become a big city chief someday until her father was accused of taking bribes and hastily retired before it could be proven. This finally freed her to stop doing what her father wanted and look at what she wanted.

Skeet has one cat—Wilma Mankiller—and a collie—Lady.
DOMINANT TRAITS= intelligent, tenacious, tough, truth-seeker, responsible (for her people)
COMPLEMENTARY TRAITS= Hot-tempered, knitter/gardener, capable and resourceful
CONTRAST= tender heart, reckless when someone's in danger

VALUES= Responsibility to all who help or whom she's given her protection—Giving credit where due, honesty, justice, fairness and equality, loyalty

She adored her father and resented her mother for leaving him and taking her away. As soon as she graduated from high school, she went to KC to attend police academy and be a cop, just like him - only to find that he didn't think she was good enough to be a cop because she was female, only to find he was a drunk, only to find he took her husband's side over hers when she left an unhappy marriage and compared her to her mother, Coreen. Reluctantly and over a long period of time, she discovered her feelings about both father and mother changing.

After she left for KC, her mother remarried and had two more children, a brother, Buddy, born when Skeet was 20 and a sister, Nancy, born when Skeet was 23.

(Many more pages and more for other characters—new page)

Outline

Chapter One

Scene 1 – Andrew's vwpt. Tom Jamison confronts Andrew about Tina in his office and threatens him. After he leaves, Andrew steals Scott's research.

Scene 2 – Stuart's vwpt. Stuart Morley meets Andrew at night at entrance to the nature preserve to pay him off for blackmail.

Scene 3 - Jeremy's vwpt. The three vice chancellors meet in Jeremy Coulter's office to discuss Andrew's blackmail threats and how to stop him.

Scene 4 - Brian's vwpt. Brian and Tina hear some gossip (from Tom?) about Andrew.

Chapter Two

Scene 1 - Skeet eats breakfast with her friends when Sam comes in and makes a huge scene and Joe has to throw him out.

Chapter Three

Scene 1 – Skeet stops by squad room.

Scene 2 – After the chancellor's staff meeting, Skeet has lunch with Annette, Mike, Tina, and Tony Morelli (maybe someone else?) in Chouteau Union. Scott and Andrew fight. Skeet and Mike separate them and make them leave.

Scene 3 – In squad room, Skeet works on mail, reports, and greets the newest recruit, Dave Parker, who'll be on patrol that night. Frank's been gone all afternoon. When he comes in late, he argues with Skeet about Janice's sexual harassment charges and about adding the *News* offices to the night rounds. Skeet leaves angry and encounters Brian waiting for Tina. She offers him a ride but he explains his mom's coming.

Scene 4 – Skeet picks up some yarn that Molly's been holding for her. Molly's got to drive into the city to see in-laws so Skeet heads over to Pyewacket's alone for supper. She runs into Joe and Julie and eats with them. They see Tina and Brian. Joe talks abut his shortage of cops and he and Skeet expand their agreement about Girlville policing.

(Many more pages—new page)

Research

Campus police procedures – H____ H_____

KCMO Police Department procedures – F_____ C_____
_Small town/county police/medical examiner procedures—
(Many more pages—new page)

Could also include any of the other documents here—Freewriting, Questions, etc.

Scenes I Want to See in *Every Hidden Fear*

(This is a sample of a 4-page document)

More with Gran, especially with traditional history/culture

Gran makes Skeet take kids to the city council meeting to witness the big fight

Skeet asks Gran to help her get grounded in her culture again

Scene where Skeet has had to fight off someone she thinks is the murderer and Gran shows up with bat or shovel or something to try to help

Another confrontation with Miryam and Walker

Terry finds out Walker's trying to railroad Noah and blows up

Human trafficking task force meeting

Meeting with KCMO tech guy to learn what's on jump drive scene

Meeting where Elizabeth B. tells Skeet she's afraid for her political career

Hints to foreshadow the relationship between Sam and Erika

Terry trying to connect with Skeet & the chemistry between them

Joe trying to push a relationship with Skeet to the point of the "friend-zone" explosion

NEED—BIG story-changing action scene for the Midpoint

Angie is forced to tell Skeet something that makes Noah look guilty to keep Brian from losing respect for her

Big confrontation/fight scene at the golf course restaurant

BIG, BIG blizzard chase scene out in the country at end

Gran makes Skeet clean out gutters and predicts blizzard when weathermen are saying no

Scene at City Market in KC

Skeet finds body on golf course on early-morning run—alone? With someone? Joe trying heavy-handed to court her

Miryam tells Skeet what Walker did to her